NB  CHECK FOR 2 PATTERNS AT BACK

£2·50

NB  CHECK FOR 2 PATTERNS AT BACK.

# CREATIVE WOOL EMBROIDERY

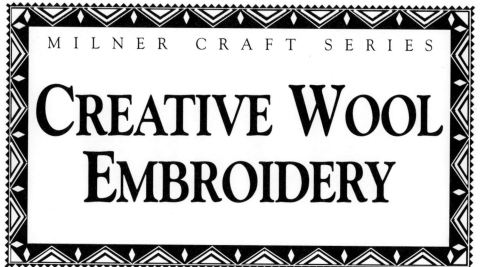

MILNER CRAFT SERIES

# CREATIVE WOOL EMBROIDERY

JOAN WATTERS

SALLY MILNER PUBLISHING

To Elizabeth Cranny, a wonderful lady who had great faith in
my designs and my embroidery.

First published in 1995 by
Sally Milner Publishing Pty Ltd
558 Darling Street
Rozelle NSW 2039 Australia

© Joan Watters, 1995 (twice)

Cover and colour pages design by Joanne Kouvaris
Design and typesetting by Associated Print Management
Photography by John Hollingshead
Photographs styled by Lisa Hilton
Illustrations by Jacqui Quennell
Back cover author photograph by Benjamin Huie
Colour separated in Australia by Sphere Color Graphics
Printed in Australia by Impact Printing

National Library of Australia
Cataloguing-in-Publication data:

Watters, Joan.
    Creative wool embroidery.

    ISBN 1 86351 163 6.

    1. Embroidery. 2. Embroidery – Patterns. 3. Embroidery –
Design. 1. Title. (Series: Milner craft series).

746.44

# CONTENTS

# ACKNOWLEDGEMENTS

This is my first book and there are many people I would like to thank. First of all, my wonderful family – my husband, John, and my children, John, Mark and Peta – for their love and support. They missed out on some attention while I was writing this book, but I know they are all proud of me.

Thank you to Elizabeth Cranny, without whose encouragement I would not have been able to complete this project. She was always there when I needed her, and she showed me that there is only one way to go now, and that is forward.

Many thanks to Sandra Kahler for her tireless typing and photocopying, and for her nagging me to get the job done. She gave much support and many hours of her time.

Margaret Palmer spent endless hours crocheting, and without her beautiful work I would not have made it. I am indebted to her for that. Heartfelt thanks also to my dear friend Su-Lee Oei for making the beautiful tassels for the needle book and chatelaine, in spite of many other demands on her time.

My daughter, Peta, did a great job stamping all the greeting cards, and Helen O'Neill, my long-time good friend, generously gave me the run of her beautiful home for the photography in this book.

Sally, Eve, Lisa and other staff members at Sally Milner Publishing have all been very helpful. I am most grateful to Sally for her confidence in my embroidery and designs, and her support during the publishing process.

I would also like to acknowledge the following businesses and thank them for their supplies:

Cheryl of Ristal Threads, Morella, RMB 4650, Tatong, Vic 3673 – for her donation of Kirra Mohair yarns;

Coral Stuart of Little Wood Fleece Yarns, Creightons Creek Road, RMB 2250, Euroa, Vic 3666 – for her donation of hand-dyed mohair wools;

Catherine Barnett of Coats Patons Crafts, 89–91 Peters Avenue, Mulgrave, Vic 3170 – for her donation of Anchor wools;

Elizabeth White of Down Under Australia, Suite 3, 559 Sydney Road, Seaforth, NSW 2092 – for her donation of various threads;

David Ireland of Ireland Needlecraft, PO Box 1175, Narre Warren, Vic 3805 – for his donation of jewellery pieces;

Sally of Sarah Sey Dolls and Crafts, 39 Annangrove Road, Kenthurst, NSW 2156 – for donating and painting the porcelain half doll.

# INTRODUCTION

Wool embroidery is perfect for people who have never embroidered before, because they will see results straight away. This is a great confidence booster. What's more, slight irregularities in stitching will not detract from the finished look of the embroidery, and it is possible to achieve beautiful results using only a few different types of stitches.

Wool embroidery is also a great way to start embroidering again, if you have somehow been put off this craft in the past. We can all remember the days when the back of our work had to look like the front. Embroidery became a tiresome bore, and many of us stopped doing it. Well, those days are over. In wool embroidery you can even tie knots, a real 'no no' in the old days. I hear the same story over and over from my students – that they love working embroidery now it is no longer vital to keep the back perfect. (If you do want to keep the back of your work the same as the front, by all means do so, but I am not going to insist on it.)

Many people have the idea that wool embroidery is only for decorating babywear. Women would often say to me, 'I would love to do your workshops but I do not have any babies'. The number of times I heard this comment made me determined to write a book on wool embroidery that had nothing to do with babies, just to dispel this notion. I have included a bear in the projects section, but it is more for decoration than for use as a baby toy. I collect bears and I am sure there are many people out there who are like me.

I have tried to vary the colours in the designs to suit a wide cross-section of tastes. I love working with colour, but my specialty is working in tone on tone. I would have to say that cream on cream is my favourite combination. However, colours are very personal, and I don't expect everyone to share my taste. It is exciting to experiment with colours, and I hope you feel free to do so.

The designs in this book are suitable for beginners and experienced embroiderers alike. There are a few challenges, but all the stitches and flowers are clearly explained, and achieving a lovely result is only a matter of following the instructions. Whatever your level of expertise, I hope that you will enjoy making the projects in this book as much as I have.

# CHAPTER 1

# EQUIPMENT AND MATERIALS

## FABRICS

Wool embroidery is best worked on woollen fabrics. I love working on 100 per cent wool blanketing, and most of the designs shown in this book are worked on this fabric. Woollen dress fabrics are suitable and wool blend fabrics can be embroidered successfully. You can embroider on thick and thin fabrics, but if the fabric is thin, consider using the finer embroidery wools.

## NEEDLES

The size of the needle will depend on the weave and thickness of the fabric, and the thickness and number of strands of thread. Test your needle out on your fabric first. If you are struggling to bring the needle through the fabric, change to a smaller or larger needle. Use a fine needle on fine fabrics and when doing fine work using one thread. However, in some of the projects in this book, I use the same size needle for thick and thin threads. You must feel comfortable with the needles you use.

Use tapestry needles on wool blanketing where possible, as they do not dig into your finger. These needles are short and heavy with long eyes and blunt points. However, you might find that you cannot use tapestry needles on some brands of blanketing. Then you should use chenille needles. You will have to experiment.

If you are embroidering on woollen dress fabric, always use a chenille needle. This large-eyed needle has a thick shaft and a sharp point.

For embroidering large numbers of twists on a bullion stitch, use a small doll needle, which will give you the length required to hold all the twists.

Needles come in a range of sizes. The larger the number of the needle, the finer it is.

## THREADS

*Wools*
I use tapestry wools, which are thick 4-ply wools; crewel wools, which are 2-ply wools; medium-weight mohair wools; and over-dyed mohair threads, dyed so that the colour varies throughout the skein.

*Other Threads*
I like to vary the textures of my designs by using threads other than wool, and today there is a great array available. I use pure silk threads; shiny rayon threads; synthetic threads to create a glittery or dull finish; fuzzy threads; stranded cotton, which comes in six strands; Perle cotton, which comes in numerous sizes, but I have used No. 3 thick and No. 5 thin; Ribbon Floss, which is a rayon ribbon; and metallic threads. The list could go on and on. Using different threads adds depth to your embroidery, so do not be frightened to experiment.

I also like to add beads to my embroidery, and Mill Hill puts out a good-quality range.

## OTHER NECESSITIES

- tracing paper
- template plastic
- water soluble pen
- lead pencil

- white marking pencil (for transferring designs to darker fabrics)
- tape measure and pins
- needle threader
- sewing thread
- sewing machine and sewing machine needles
- toy filling
- craft glue
- Fray Stopper
- braids, laces and other trims

Check the 'Requirements' list before starting any of the projects.

# Chapter 2

# HINTS AND TECHNIQUES

### Transferring Designs

This is a simple procedure. Take a piece of tracing paper the size of the design, or the size of one section if the design is a large one. Using a pencil, mark the centre of each flower with a dot, and dot in any lines in the design. You can also mark the flower outlines if you wish. Now use a needle to poke a hole where you have made each dot.

Place the tracing onto the fabric. It is a good idea to pin the tracing paper to the fabric when transferring the design, to prevent movement.

Take a water soluble pen (not a pencil) and mark the fabric through the holes. You will end up with a series of dots representing the flowers and other elements in the design. Mark each section in this manner.

The water soluble pen markings can be removed easily by damping the design area with cold water.

### Working the Embroidery

- Use a needle threader to make the job of threading the needle easier. I use a metal threader rather than a wire one. If you don't have a needle threader, flatten the wool by folding it over the eye of the needle. Now thread the flattened section.

- In all my wool embroidery I start with a knot and then take a small back stitch to secure the thread. If the knot is not secured, it can come through the fabric. (It is very hard to keep the back of your work neat with wool embroidery, so it is usual to line wool-embroidered items. If you wish to try to keep the back tidy, by all means do so.) Now you are ready to start your design.

- The one thing you have to remember with wool embroidery is that it is worked loose. If you pull the embroidery too tight, you will not be able to achieve the raised look in your work. I also work a little looser on my ordinary embroidery now, as I think it gives a better result.

### Laundering

I am a little old-fashioned when it comes to washing, and always wash delicates by hand. Use a soft wool wash solution. The most important part of washing delicates is removing the soap solution. I always rinse my delicates at least three times and even then, if I think the soap is not removed, I will rinse again. I also drip dry my delicates. This may take a little longer but the results make the effort worthwhile. Lay delicates on a towel to dry once most of the excess water has drained away.

It is important to iron wool embroidery correctly. Incorrect ironing can ruin many hours of hard work. Place a clean white or cream towel on the ironing board. The towel acts as a cushion. Place the embroidery right side down into the towel and place a piece of cotton fabric over the wrong side of the embroidery. Make sure the heat setting on the iron is not up too high. Always do a test iron first on a scrap of fabric. Gently iron the cotton fabric covering the embroidery.

# CHAPTER 3

# FLOWER GUIDE

This chapter provides you with instructions on how to embroider the flowers used in the designs featured in the book.

The symbols used in the design charts can be found at the end of this chapter.

### WOOL ROSE

- 1st row – Work five satin stitches, 4 mm (just under $1/4$") in length, close together (diag. 1). Work seven satin stitches close together over the top of the first five. The stitch length this time is 12 mm ($1/2$"). Extend the length of the stitch on one side only (diag. 2).

- 2nd row – Bring the needle up at any corner (corner A on diag. 3), take it down at the opposite corner B and then back up at A – all in the one movement (diag. 3A). Take the needle back down a little below B, creating a slight angle on the stitch, and then up again at A (diag. 3B). Once again this stitch should be worked all in the one movement (push the needle from one point to the other). Work the next stitch a little below the last stitch, but this time go straight down at B (diag. 3C). Bring the needle up at corner B and begin the next set of three stitches (diag. 3D). Working in a clockwise direction, repeat the previous instructions three more times so that you cover the four corners (diag. 4).

- 3rd row – This final step is very important, as it makes a square rose into a round rose. Take a large stem stitch, but instead of keeping the wool in a back position, keep it on the top of the rose. This method gives the rose a fluffy look. Work this row in an anti-clockwise direction (diag. 5). The size of the stitches is 12 mm ($1/2$"), but you do not have to measure the size of every stitch. Take an even amount with the needle, 4 mm (almost $1/4$"), front and back to the previous stitch. This means you are moving around the same amount each stitch. When you return to where you started, you must go two stitches past the start to make the rose look even.

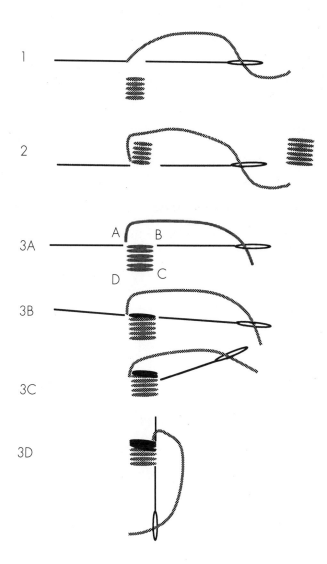

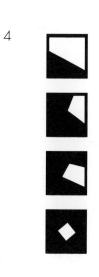

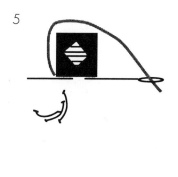

## WOOL ROSE BUD

- 1st row – Embroider one fly stitch and one straight stitch using the darkest colour. Do not make the space between the spokes of the fly stitch too large, as the straight stitch must fit snugly inside the fly stitch (diag. 1).

- 2nd row – Work one fly stitch around the first row using the lightest colour (diag. 2).

- 3rd row – Embroider one fly stitch around the first and second rows using the green wool, and extend the fly stitch to form the stem of the bud. At the top of the bud, embroider two straight stitches in the shape of a V facing away from the bud (diag. 3).

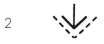

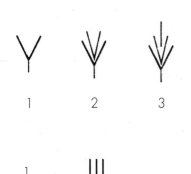

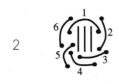

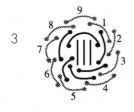

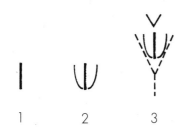

### WOOL ROSE LEAVES

- 1st row – Embroider one fly stitch with a small gap in between the spokes (diag. 1).

- 2nd row – Embroider a fly stitch above the first fly stitch. Make the gap between the spokes smaller again (diag. 2).

- 3rd row – Embroider a straight stitch in the gap of the previous fly stitch.

### LARGE BULLION ROSE

The secret of a bullion rose is keep the stitches as close as possible. The distance between A and B (see diag. 1 on page 16) on this rose is 10 mm ($^3/8$"). Use 11 twists on all petals.

- 1st row – Work three bullion stitches very close together (diag. 1).

- 2nd row – Work six bullion stitches, starting at 1 and then going from outside in for bullions 2, 3, 4 and 5. Number 6 bullion sits outside. (See diag. 2 for positions.)

- 3rd row – Work nine bullions for this row, starting at 1 and then going from outside in for bullions 2, 3, 4, 5, 6, 7 and 8. Number 9 bullion sits outside. (See diag. 3 for positions.)

### LARGE BULLION ROSE BUD

- 1st row – The centre bullion has 12 twists (diag. 1).

- 2nd row – The bullions each side of the centre bullion have 10 twists each (diag. 2).

- 3rd row – Work a fly stitch around the bullion bud and extend the holding stitch back to the rose. At the top of the bud, embroider two straight stitches in the shape of a V facing away from the bud (diag. 3).

### SMALL BULLION ROSE

These roses are used on the Jewellery Box Lid and the Pendant. Work these roses in the same way as the large bullion roses, but use finer wool and only 6 twists. The distance between A and B (see diag. 1 on page 16) on this rose is 5 mm ($^1/4$"). Work the same number of petals and three rows of petals, as for the large bullion rose.

Check instructions for the wool colours, and use a No. 20 chenille needle for the bullion stitch.

### SMALL BULLION ROSE LEAVES

These are used on the Jewellery Box Lid and the Pendant. Work these leaves in the same manner as the wool rose leaves, only use finer wool and embroider them much smaller.

### TINY BULLION ROSE

Tiny bullion roses are used for the brooch and earrings, and therefore have to be worked very small. The distance between A and B (see diag. 1 on page 16) is 3 mm ($1/8$").

- 1st row – Work one bullion stitch using the darkest colour and 4 twists only (diag. 1).

- 2nd row – Work four bullion stitches in this row, still using only 4 twists (diag. 2). Use the second colour for this row.

- 3rd row – In this row, work six to eight bullion stitches, depending on your tension, but still use only 4 twists (diag. 3).

### TINY BULLION ROSE LEAVES

Embroider one tiny fly stitch and one straight stitch in the gap in the spokes of the fly stitch. Make the gap very small so that the straight stitch fits snugly inside.

### CAMELLIA

The camellias are worked in bullion stitch. Check on how to embroider bullion stitch in the stitch guide.

To make a camellia petal, wind 30 twists around a 10 cm (4") doll needle. Do not wind the twists too tightly. The distance between A and B for the camellias is 12 mm ($1/2$"). (See diag. 1 on page 16.) Once you have the 30 twists on your needle, ease them off and even the twists down the thread. These petals will take a little longer to do than the normal bullion stitch and a little more patience, but the end result is beautiful.

- Draw a circle the same size as diagram 1.

- Work the first row of petals. This consists of five petals overlapping one another (diag. 2). The look you would have if you were embroidering the petals in a straight line is shown in diagram 3.

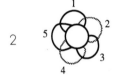

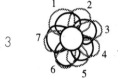

- Embroider the second row of petals at the back of the first row. The petals in the second row have the same amount of twists and the petals also overlap each other (diag. 4). The number of petals in this row will depend on your tension. I usually manage seven or eight petals.

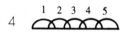

- Fill the centre of the camellia with colonial knots (diag. 5).

### CAMELLIA LEAVES

Work the leaves in continuous fly stitch. Embroider a straight stitch in the centre of the top fly stitch. Check the design as to how many fly stitches you need to embroider first, and always start away from the camellia flower.

## STEM STITCH ROSE

These roses are embroidered on the Elegant Doll Pin Cushion, Needle Book and Chatelaine. An important point to remember with the roses in these designs is that they are worked very small. I would suggest you have a practice run on a scrap of fabric before you start these projects.

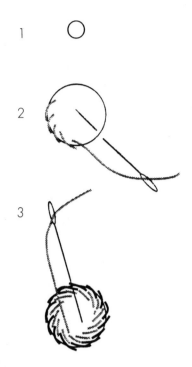

1

2

3

- Draw a very small circle, no bigger than that shown in diagram 1, with a water soluble pen. This marks the centre of the rose.

- Using a single strand of Kirra yarns Mohair in the colour mentioned in the instructions, start with a knot and a back stitch to secure the knot. Work in stem stitch but keep the stitches very loose. You will have a loop on the right side of your work. Work stem stitches around the circle until it is full (diag. 2).

- Even though it may seem impossible, you will be able to fit another small row of stem stitches inside this outer circle (diag. 3).

- To finish off the flower, take the thread down through the centre of the rose, but leave the loop loose. Finish the thread off at the back of the work, but be careful not to pull the loop tightly.

## BUTTONHOLE FLOWERS, BUDS AND VINES

*Flowers*_____
Follow the instructions for buttonhole stitch, and make the flowers a complete circle.

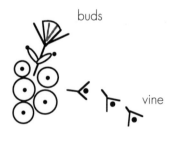

buds

vine

buttonhole flowers

*Buds*_____
- Follow the instructions for buttonhole stitch, but this time embroider only four stitches. Embroider one fly stitch with a stem around each bud in green.

- At the base of the stem embroider two lazy daisy leaves in green. Some designs, especially the Crazy Wool Embroidery on page 62, will have more than two leaves. Please read the instructions and check the designs for the number of leaves.

*Vine* _____
The vine consists of colonial knots with one fly stitch and a short stem in green around each knot.

## STRAIGHT STITCH FLOWER

This flower is very simple to embroider but it looks great. Each petal consists of two straight stitches on top of one another. The flowers are worked in three colours.

The most difficult part of working this flower is achieving five evenly placed petals. The petals should be drawn in before you start to embroider. An easy way to mark the petals is to draw a Y and then add one petal each side in the space, as in the diagram.

- 1st row – Embroider two petals in the colour specified in the instructions.

- 2nd row – Embroider three petals in the second colour specified.

- 3rd row – Embroider one colonial knot in the centre of the flower in the third colour specified in the instructions.

## PISTIL STITCH FLOWER

Check the stitch guide on how to embroider pistil stitch. You should wind 2 twists around the needle for the petals.

- Mark a small circle in the centre of the flower for the colonial knots.

- 1st row – The petal positions are shown in diagram 1.

- 2nd row – The petals this time do not begin at the inner circle, but instead start halfway along the first row of petals (diag. 2). This gives them the appearance of being longer, but they should be kept the same length.

- Fill the centre of the flower with colonial knots.

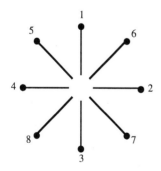

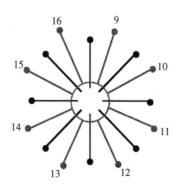

## CONTINUOUS FLY STITCH FERN

Follow instructions for continuous fly stitch on page 18.

## LAVENDER

- 1st row – Work one lazy daisy stitch at the centre. Then embroider a lazy daisy stitch on each side of the first, both facing outwards (diag. 1).

- 2nd row – Below the first three petals, embroider two more lazy daisy stitches facing inwards (diag. 2).

- 3rd row – Embroider one lazy daisy stitch below and centred between the previous two petals (diag. 3).

- 4th row – Embroider two colonial knots below the last petal. (See diag. 4 for positions.)

- 5th row – Embroider one straight stitch above the petals to form the stem (diag. 5).

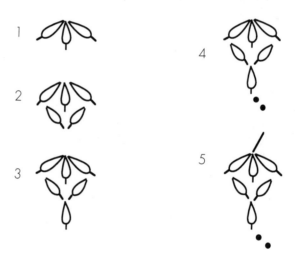

## GOLDEN WATTLE BLOSSOM

- Embroider stems and leaves in stem stitch using Appletons crewel wool No. 644.

- Work blossom in colonial knots, some in DMC Perle 3 No. 726 and some in DMC Perle 3 No. 727. Use both colours in the one blossom bunch.

- Add a few colonial knots in Charleston thread No. 412. This thread will give the wattle a sparkle.

## TEA-TREE FLOWER

- Work petals in lazy daisy stitch using Semco wool No. 424. Work tips of petals in fly stitch using Appletons crewel wool No. 944 (diag. 1).

- Work leaves in continuous fly stitch and Appletons crewel wool No. 644.

- Work bud in lazy daisy stitch and Semco tapestry wool No. 424 (diag. 3). Work the bud tip in fly stitch and Appletons crewel wool No. 944. There is a colonial knot at the end of the bud. Use one strand of Appletons crewel wool No. 944 and one strand of No. 644 together.

- The knots in the centre of the flower are worked in the same wool as the knot at the end of the bud.

- Work a fly stitch for the leaf around the bud, taking the stem back to the flower. Use Appletons crewel wool No. 644.

 1
 2
 3

## FLANNEL FLOWER

- Work the petals in lazy daisy stitch and Semco wool No. 472. Work the tips of petals in fly stitch using Semco wool No. 475 split into two threads. Do not have the thread too long when you are splitting.

- The centre of the flower consists of seven colonial knots in Semco wool No. 475.

- The leaves are worked in fly stitch and straight stitch using Semco wool No. 475 split into two.

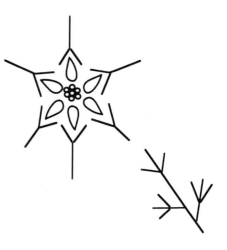

## WARATAH FLOWER

- Draw the top of the waratah first from the design you are following. The top of the waratah is completely covered with colonial knots in Semco wool No 417 (diag. 1).

- Work the first row of petals in large lazy daisy with a longer anchoring stitch and a straight stitch in the centre. Use Semco wool No. 419.

- Work the second row of petals the same as above, but go in between the petals of the row before (diag. 2). Use Appletons tapestry wool No. 505.

- The leaves are straight stitches in Semco wool No. 493. The veins of leaves are straight stitches and fly stitch, in Appletons crewel wool No. 406 (diag. 3).

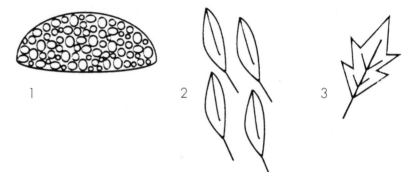

## STURT'S DESERT PEA

- Each petal is a large lazy daisy stitch with a longer anchoring stitch. Work a straight stitch in the centre. Use Semco wool No. 418.

- Work colonial knots for the centres of the flowers using Semco wool No. 458.

- The stems are in stem stitch and Appletons crewel wool No. 406.

- Work the fly stitch leaves in Semco wool No. 493 (diag. 2).

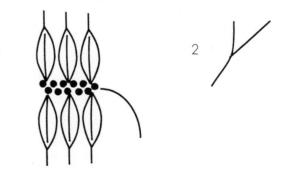

### LEMON GUM BLOSSOM

- Work the stems in stem stitch and Appletons crewel wool No. 295. Also work the leaves and veins in stem stitch and Appletons crewel wool No. 295.

- Work the flower pod in buttonhole stitch and Appletons crewel wool No. 406.

- Work the flower blossoms in pistil stitch:
  1st row – Appletons crewel wool No. 996.
  2nd row, in between the first row – Appletons crewel wool No. 841.

### BUMBLE BEE

The bumble bee can be placed wherever you like. I placed my bee on my waratah.

- The body of the bee is satin stitch in DMC Perle 3 No. 726. The stripes on the bee's body are in straight stitch and DMC stranded cotton No. 310 using six strands.

- The wings of the bee are in bullion stitch, about 30 twists. Make four bullion wings using one strand only of Stonehouse Paterna wool No. 262.

- Work the feelers in straight stitch with a colonial knot at the end of each stitch. Use three threads only of DMC stranded cotton No. 310.

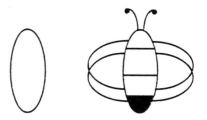

## KEY TO FLOWER SYMBOLS

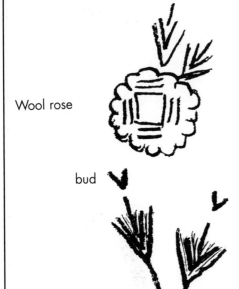

Wool rose

bud

leaves

Tiny bullion rose

leaves

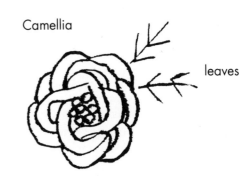

Camellia

leaves

Large bullion rose

bud

Stem stitch rose

Small bullion rose

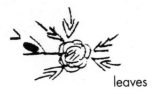

leaves

Buttonhole flower

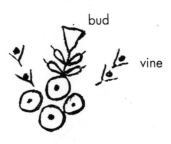

bud

vine

Straight stitch flower

Sturt's desert pea

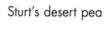

Pistil stitch flower

Lemon gum blossom

Golden wattle blossom

Continuous fly stitch fern

Lazy daisy flower

Tea-tree flower

Lavender

Flannel flower

Forget-me-nots

Waratah flower

Sunflower leaves

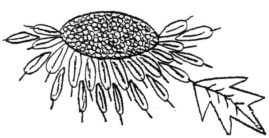

Bumble bee

Chapter 4

# STITCH GUIDE

## BACK STITCH

- Bring the needle up through the fabric at A (which is one stitch length from the start of the work).

- Insert the needle at B, and then bring it up again at C.

- Continue inserting the needle into the end of the last stitch and bringing it out one stitch ahead.

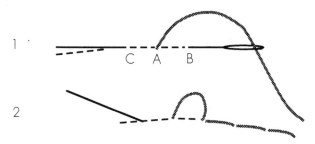

## BULLION STITCH

- Bring the needle and thread up through the fabric at A and insert the needle at B. (The distance between A and B will vary according to the flower being worked.)

- Bring the needle up again at A. Pull the needle part of the way through the fabric, but do not bring the eye through.

- Start winding the thread around the point of the needle. Do not wind the thread too tightly. The number of twists depends on the flower you are doing. When you have the required amount of twists on the needle, hold the twists gently and pull the needle though them.

- Make sure the twists are evenly spaced down the thread. Reinsert the needle and thread at B, and pull through the fabric.

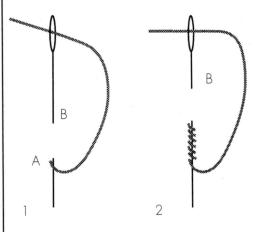

## BUTTONHOLE STITCH

- Mark the centre point, A, and bring the needle up though the fabric at B.

- Insert the needle at A and come out again with the thread below the needle beside B. Pull the needle out to form the stitch.

- Continue in this manner, working from left to right. Insert the needle at A all the time, but move around at B to form a circle or half-circle, depending on which flower you are working.

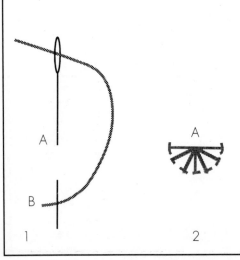

### CHAIN STITCH

- Bring the needle up at A. Make a loop with the thread on the surface of the fabric, and hold it in place with your left thumb.

- Insert the needle again at A and bring the needle out at B. Keep the thread under the point of the needle, thus maintaining the loop. Pull the thread, but not tightly.

- Repeat this process again, only this time come up at B.

- When you have completed the required number of chain stitches, end the last stitch with a stitch over the loop.

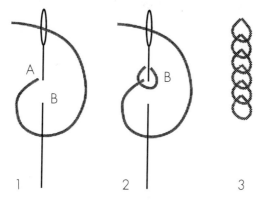

### WHIPPED CHAIN STITCH

- Embroider the chain stitch first.

- Bring the needle up through the fabric at A. Leading with the eye of the needle, slide the needle under the chain stitch, but do not go though the fabric. Pull the thread, but not tightly.

- Continue sliding the needle and thread under each chain stitch until you reach the end. Take the thread through to the back of the fabric, and end off.

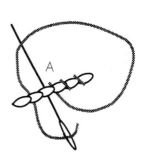

### COLONIAL KNOT

- Bring the needle up through the fabric at A.

- Place your left hand under the thread, and pass the needle under the thread, from left to right (diag. 1).

- Now lift the thread up and over the needle from left to right, forming a figure of eight (diag. 2).

- Insert the needle into the fabric very near to where the thread came up first and pull the knot down the needle. Pull the needle and thread though the fabric, making sure you hold the knot as you pull through.

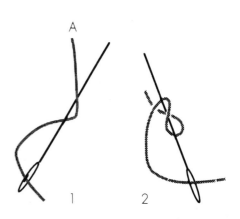

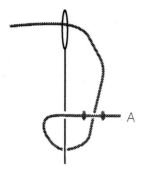

## CORAL STITCH

- Working from right to left, bring the needle up at A. Lay the thread down to the left over the line to be followed.

- Take a small stitch towards you with the thread over and around the needle. Pull the needle and thread through to form a knot.

- Continue taking stitches the same distance apart to form the stem.

## FEATHER STITCH

Feather stitch is one stitch to the left and one stitch to the right of the line to be covered. The stitch itself is like a fly stitch, without the anchoring stitch.

- Bring the needle up at A, at the top of the line to be followed.

- Take the needle across the line to the right and into the fabric at B. Come out of the fabric again at C, looping the thread under the needle as in fly stitch.

- Repeat the same stitch, this time to the left of the line.

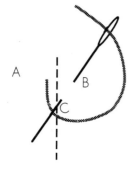
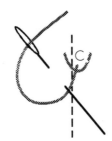
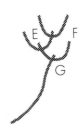

## FLY STITCH

Fly stitch can be used for flowers, leaves and trimming other flowers.

- Bring the needle up through the fabric at A. Then insert the needle the required distance to the right of A, at B. Bring the needle out halfway between A and B, at C.

- Anchor the loop with a straight stitch, taking the needle to the back of the work at D. The length of this stitch can vary according to the flower or leaves you are working.

To work continuous fly stitch, follow instructions for fly stitch, but instead of finishing off each stitch, join on another stitch.

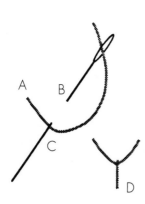

### LADDER STITCH

Ladder stitch is used to close openings or for sewing on ears. It is basically a small running stitch.

- Take one tiny stitch on the seam line of the top opening and then one stitch on the seam line of the bottom opening. Pull the thread firmly. The raw edges will turn inside.

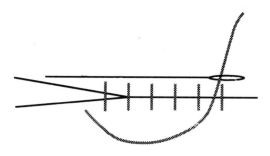

### LAZY DAISY STITCH

- Bring the needle up through the fabric at the inside of the petal, at A. Insert the needle back at B, and bring it up again just outside the tip of the petal, at C. The length of the petal will depend on the type of flower you are working.

- Loop the thread around the needle and pull the needle and thread through the fabric.

- Anchor the loop with a tiny straight stitch at the tip of the petal. This stitch can vary in length.

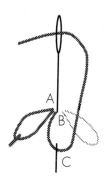

### PISTIL STITCH

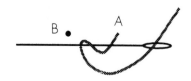

- Bring the needle up through the fabric at A. Hold the needle horizontal and wind the thread around the needle once or twice, according to the flower you are doing.

- Turn the needle towards the fabric and insert it at B, about 5 mm ($^1$/4") from A. Hold the knot in place as you pull the needle and thread through the fabric.

### SATIN STITCH

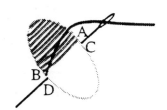

Satin stitches are straight stitches worked side by side. Work them close together to cover the fabric well.

- Bring the needle up at A and take it down at B. Use a stabbing motion for better tension.

- Work the second stitch, from C to D, as close to the first stitch as possible.

### STEM STITCH

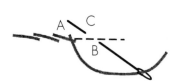

Work this stitch from left to right with small stitches all the same length.

- Bring the needle up at A and take it down at B.

- Then bring it up at C, just above the previous stitch, making sure the thread is always on the bottom of the needle.

### STRAIGHT STITCH

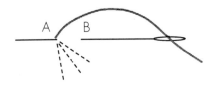

- Bring the needle up at A and take it down at B. Be careful not to pull the thread too tightly.

# Chapter 5

# SIMPLE DESIGNS

Each version of the following designs is shown on a particular item in the colour pages. For example, Version 1 of the first design has been worked on a lingerie bag. Sewing instructions for all the items appear in Chapter 6. You can apply the design to the item suggested or mix and match.

In most of the following designs, I have used no more than one skein of each of the threads. The amount of thread required will depend on your tension and the size of the flowers you are working. Buy one skein of each thread to start with and purchase more if you require it.

The embroidery design charts tell you how many leaves and flowers you will require and also the positioning of each section. Note that not all the design charts are full size. You will have to enlarge some of them on a photocopier by punching in the percentages given.

To embroider the flowers and other elements of the designs, refer to the flower and stitch guides at all times.


## WOOL ROSE BOUQUET WITH CREAM BOW

*Version 1 – shown on Lingerie Bag* _____

REQUIREMENTS
**Materials:**
Wool blanketing, 60 cm x 38 cm (23 $^1/2$" x 15")
No. 18 tapestry needles (or No. 18 chenille needles if tapestry
   unsuitable)
No. 9 crewel needles
Small pearl beads
Cream sewing thread to match the blanketing

**Threads:**
DMC Perle 5 No. 712
Appletons tapestry wool
– Nos 715, 714, 711 and 356

**Stitches used:**
Satin stitch, fly stitch, straight stitch, continuous fly stitch, coral stitch and stem stitch.

1. Transfer the design chart on page 22 onto your fabric (see page 3).

2. Using DMC Perle 5 No.712, embroider the bow in satin stitch.

3. Embroider the wool roses:
   1st row – Appletons tapestry wool No. 715.
   2nd row – Appletons tapestry wool No. 714.
   3rd row – Appletons tapestry wool No. 711.

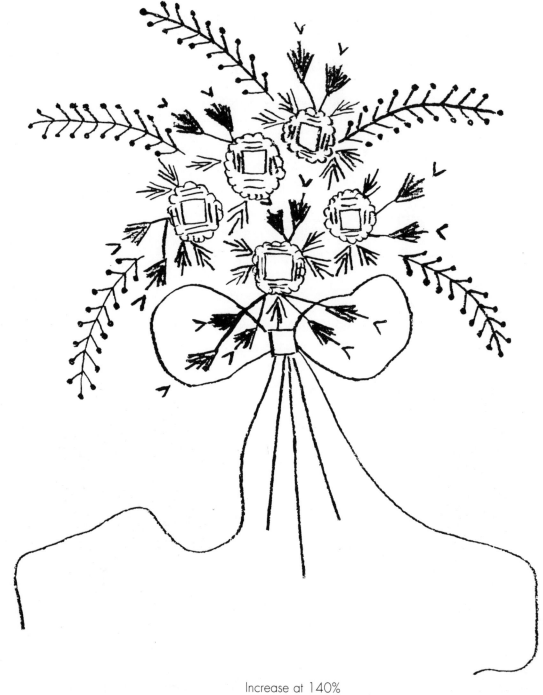

Increase at 140%

Rose Bouquet with Cream Bow – Version 1

4. Embroider the rose leaves next using Appletons tapestry wool No. 356.

5. Embroider the rose buds:
   1st row – Appletons tapestry wool No. 715.
   2nd row – Appletons tapestry wool No. 711.
   3rd row – Appletons tapestry wool No. 356.

6. Embroider the fly stitch fern, using DMC Perle 5 No. 712 and continuous fly stitch.
   Using a No. 9 crewel needle and cream sewing thread, sew pearl beads on the tips of the fly stitches.

7. Embroider the stems in coral stitch using Appletons tapestry wool No. 356.

See page 42 for instructions on how to make up a lingerie bag.

*Version 2 – shown on Wooden Coathanger Cover*

To work the design, you will need a piece of wool blanketing, 56 cm x 38 cm (22 $^1$/$_2$" x 15"), plus the other materials and threads listed for Version 1.

First trace the design chart below. Now follow the instructions for Version 1 above, steps 2 to 7.

To make up the coathanger cover, follow the instructions on page 45.

Version 2 – increase at 140%

Greeting Card – increase at 140%

Rose Bouquet with Cream Bow

*Version 3 – shown on Greeting Card*

To work the design, you will need a small piece of woollen fabric, 12 cm x 16 cm (4 ³/₄" x 6 ¹/₄"), and the needles and threads listed for Version 1. If you have worked on either Version 1 or 2 of this design, you should have enough threads left over.

Using a water soluble pen, draw the outline of the opening in the card on the piece of woollen fabric. This outline shows you how far out you can take the embroidery. Now trace the design chart on page 23. Follow the instructions for Version 1 of this design, steps 2 to 7.

See page 49 for instructions on how to make up a greeting card.

## WOOL ROSES AND BUTTONHOLE FLOWERS

*Version 1 – shown on Door Stop*

REQUIREMENTS
**Materials:**
Circle of wool blanketing, 35 cm (13 ³/₄") in diameter
No. 18 tapestry needles (or No. 18 chenille needles if tapestry unsuitable)

**Threads:**
Anchor tapestry wool
– Nos 8242, 8306, 8294 and 9176
DMC Perle 5 No. 948
Appletons crewel wool
– Nos 208 and 544
Anchor stranded cotton No. 20
DMC Medici No. 8610

**Stitches used:**
Satin stitch, stem stitch, fly stitch, straight stitch, colonial knots, buttonhole stitch, lazy daisy stitch, running stitch and ladder stitch.

1. Transfer the embroidery design on page 25 to the fabric (see page 3).

2. Embroider the wool roses first:
   1st row – Anchor tapestry wool No. 8242.
   2nd row – Anchor tapestry wool No. 8306.
   3rd row – Anchor tapestry wool No. 8294.

3. Embroider the rose leaves using Anchor tapestry wool No. 9176. Then start on the buds:
   1st row – Anchor tapestry wool No. 8242.
   2nd row – Anchor tapestry wool No. 8306.
   3rd row – Anchor tapestry wool No. 9176.

Increase at 140%

Wool Roses and Buttonhole Flowers – Version 1

4. Embroider the forget-me-nots:
Outside – colonial knots, Anchor tapestry wool No. 8294.
Centre – one colonial knot per flower, DMC Perle 5 No. 948.

5. Next embroider the buttonhole flowers in Appletons crewel wool No. 208. Once you have completed the buttonhole flowers embroider the buds using Anchor stranded thread No. 20 (6 strands). Now start on the vines using Anchor stranded cotton No. 20 and Appletons crewel wool No. 544.

6. Embroider the straight stitch flowers:
Three petals – Anchor tapestry wool No. 8242.
Two petals – Anchor tapestry wool No. 8306.
Centre – colonial knot, Anchor tapestry wool No. 8294.

7. Lavender is always embroidered last as it fills up the gaps. It is not necessary to use a lavender colour. Work as follows:
Petals – DMC Perle 5 No. 948.
Stems – DMC Medici No. 8610.

To make up the door stop, refer to instructions on page 49.

*Version 2 – shown on Greeting Card*

To work this design, you will need a piece of wool blanketing, 15 cm x 11.5 cm (6" x 4 1/2"), plus the materials and threads listed for Version 1. If you have made Version 1, you should have enough threads left over to complete this design. You will not need the DMC Medici No. 8610.

On the piece of wool fabric draw the outline of the opening in the card with a water soluble pen. Trace the design chart below. Now follow the instructions above, steps 2 to 5.

To make up the greeting card, follow steps 1, 2 and 3 on page 49. With this design I have used flat gold lace instead of pregathered lace. I did not use a ribbon bow on this card.

Actual size

**Wool Roses and Buttonhole Flowers – Greeting Card**

## WOOL-EMBROIDERED HEART

*Version 1 – shown on Lingerie Bag*

REQUIREMENTS

**Materials:**
Wool blanketing, 60 cm x 38 cm (23 1/2" x 15")
No. 18 tapestry needles (or No. 18 chenille needles if tapestry unsuitable)
No. 9 crewel needles
Cream sewing thread to match wool blanketing
2 gold hearts

**Threads:**
Stonehouse Paterna wool No. 263
DMC Perle 5 ecru
Appletons tapestry wool No. 992
DMC Perle 3 ecru
Charleston thread No. 416

**Stitches used:**
Continuous fly stitch, colonial knots, bullion stitch, fly stitch, straight stitch, lazy daisy stitch and pistil stitch.

1. Trace the heart first from the design chart on page 28 with a water soluble pen (see page 3).

2. Embroider one side of the heart and then reverse the stitching for the second half. The heart is embroidered in continuous fly stitch using one strand of Stonehouse Paterna wool No. 263.

3. Embroider the colonial knots on the continuous fly stitch next using DMC Perle 5 ecru.

4. Embroider the bullion rose using Appletons tapestry wool No. 992, and 11 twists for the bullion. Check the large bullion rose instructions in the flower and stitch guides.

5. Embroider the rose leaves, also using Appletons tapestry wool No. 992.

6. Embroider the bullion buds:
   1st row – centre bullion, 12 twists, DMC Perle 3 ecru.
   2nd row – bullions each side of the centre bullion, 10 twists each, DMC Perle 3 ecru.
   3rd row – fly stitch around the bullion bud, Appletons tapestry wool No. 992.

7. Embroider the lazy daisy flowers:
   Petals – Appletons tapestry wool No. 992.
   Centres – 3 colonial knots, DMC Perle 3 ecru.
   Leaves – 2 lazy daisy stitches, DMC Perle 5 ecru.

template

Increase at 140%

Wool-embroidered Heart – Version 1

template

Increase at 140%

Wool-embroidered Heart – Version 2

8. Embroider the pistil stitch fan next, using Charleston thread No. 416:
   1st row – 5 pistil stitches in a fan.
   2nd row – 2 lazy daisy leaves in the same thread.

9. With a piece of double sewing cotton, sew the gold hearts to the bottom of the pistil stitch fan.

To make up the lingerie bag, follow instructions on page 42.

*Version 2 – shown on Wooden Coathanger Cover*

To work the design, you will need a piece of wool blanketing, 56 cm x 38 cm (22 $^1/_2$" x 15"), plus the other materials and threads listed for Version 1.

First trace the heart from the design chart on page 29. Now follow the instructions for Version 1 above, steps 2 to 9.

To make up the coathanger cover, follow the instructions on page 45.

*Version 3 – shown on Greeting Card*

To work this design, you will need a piece of wool blanketing, 12 cm x 16 cm (4 $^3/_4$" x 6 $^1/_4$"), plus the needles and threads listed for Version 1. If you have made Version 1 or 2 above, you should have enough wools left over to complete this design. You will not need the Charleston thread.

Trace the design chart with a water soluble pen. Now follow steps 4 to 7 in the instructions for Version 1 above. Then embroider the fern in continuous fly stitch using Stonehouse Paterna wool No. 263. Finally, embroider the colonial knots on the continuous fly stitch fern using DMC Perle 5 ecru.

To make up the greeting card, refer to the instructions given on page 49.

Increase at 120%

**Wool-embroidered Heart – Greeting Card**

## AUSTRALIAN WILDFLOWERS

For the flowers used in this design, check at all times with the flower guide. This will tell you which colours and stitches are needed for each of the Australian flowers.

*Version 1 – shown on Lingerie Bag*

REQUIREMENTS
**Materials:**
Wool blanketing, 60 cm x 38 cm (23 $^1/_2$" x 15")
No. 18 tapestry needles (or No. 18 chenille needles if tapestry unsuitable)

Increase at 140%

Australian Wildflowers – Version 1

**Threads:**
Semco tapestry wool
– Nos 417, 419, 493, 472, 475, 424, 418 and 458
Appletons tapestry wool No. 505
Appletons crewel wool
– Nos 406, 944, 644, 295, 996 and 841
DMC Perle 3
– Nos 726 and 727
Charleston thread No. 412
DMC stranded cotton No. 310
Stonehouse Paterna wool No. 262

**Stitches used:**
Colonial knots, lazy daisy stitch, straight stitch, fly stitch, stem stitch, buttonhole stitch, pistil stitch, satin stitch and bullion stitch.

1. Transfer the design chart on page 31 with a water soluble pen to the blanketing (see page 3).

2. Embroider the waratah flower and leaves first.

3. Embroider the flannel flowers and leaves.

4. Embroider the tea-tree flowers and leaves.

5. Embroider the Sturt's desert pea and leaves.

6. Embroider the golden wattle blossom and leaves.

7. Embroider the lemon gum blossom and leaves.

8. Finally, embroider the bumble bee.

To make up the lingerie bag, refer to the instructions on page 42. Note that the lace on the Australian Wildflowers lingerie bag does not have to be gathered (step 3).

*Version 2 – shown on Wire Coathanger Cover* _____

To work the design, you will need a piece of wool blanketing, 45 cm x 50 cm (17 3/4" x 19 3/4"), plus the needles and threads listed for Version 1.

Trace the design chart on page 33 with a water soluble pen. Now follow instructions for Version 1 above, steps 2 to 8.

To make up the wire coathanger cover, follow the instructions on page 48.

*Version 3 – shown on Greeting Card* _____

REQUIREMENTS
**Materials:**
Wool blanketing, 15 cm x 12 cm (6" x 4 3/4")
Cream braid, enough to go around opening of card plus small overlap
Cream double-sided satin ribbon, 25 cm (10") x 5 mm (1/4") wide

Increase at 180%

Australian Wildflowers – Version 2

**Threads:**
Semco tapestry wool
– Nos 417, 419, 472, 475 and 424
Appletons crewel wool
– Nos 944 and 644
DMC Perle 3
– Nos 726 and 727
Charleston thread No. 412

On the piece of woollen fabric draw with the water soluble pen the outline of the opening in the card. Trace the design chart below with a water soluble pen. Now follow steps 2, 3, 4 and 6 in the instructions for Version 1 above.

To make up the greeting card, refer to the instructions on page 49, steps 1, 2 and 3 only. Then glue a piece of cream braid around the opening on the front of the card. Tie a small bow out of the satin ribbon and glue the bow over the join in the braid.

Increase at 120%

Australian Wildflowers – Greeting Card

### LAVENDER AND BULLION ROSES

*Version 1 – shown on Beret*

REQUIREMENTS
**Materials:**
Navy beret purchased from a department store
No. 18 chenille needles
Nos 9 and 10 crewel needles
Mill Hill glass pebble beads No. 5270
Mill Hill antique glass beads No. 3028

**Threads:**
Anchor tapestry wool
– Nos 8740, 8738, 8734 and 8880
DMC Perle 3 No. 930
DMC Perle 5 No. 501
Kirra yarns Mohair No. 434
Charleston thread No. 408
Wisper 80% Kid mohair + 20% Nylon No. W93
DMC Medici No. 8308
DMC stranded cotton No. 501

**Stitches used:**
Bullion stitch, fly stitch, straight stitch, stem stitch, lazy daisy stitch, colonial knots and continuous fly stitch.

1. Transfer the design chart on page 36 to the beret (see page 3). Use a white marker on the dark fabric.

2. Embroider the large bullion roses, using 11 twists:
   1st row – Anchor tapestry wool No. 8740.
   2nd row – Anchor tapestry wool No. 8738.
   3rd row – Anchor tapestry wool No. 8734.

3. Embroider the rose leaves next using Anchor tapestry wool No. 8880.

4. Embroider the rose buds:
   1st row – centre bullion, 12 twists, DMC Perle 3 No. 930.
   2nd row – bullions each side of centre bullion, 10 twists each, DMC Perle 3 No. 930.
   3rd row – fly stitch around bullion bud and take stem back to the rose, Anchor tapestry wool No. 8880.

5. Embroider the berry stems using stem stitch and DMC Perle 5 No. 501.

6. Embroider the leaves in lazy daisy stitch using DMC Perle 5 No. 501.

7. Embroider the lazy daisy flowers using Kirra yarns Mohair No. 434.

8. Embroider the centres of the lazy daisy flowers. Each centre consists of one colonial knot in Charleston thread No. 108.

9. Embroider the continuous fly stitch fern next using Charleston thread No. 108.

10. Embroider the lavender using Wisper No. W93. Stems of lavender consist of one fly stitch in DMC Medici No. 8308.

11. Next make the berries. This method was taught to me by Jane Nicholas. Use a No. 10 crewel needle and a 127 cm (50") length of DMC stranded cotton No. 501. From the six strands, take one strand at a time and make a berry.

Increase at 130%

**Version 1 – Beret**

Increase at 130%

Version 2 – Scarf

Lavender and Bullion Roses

Thread the cotton in the needle through the hole in one of the pebble beads, leaving about 20 cm (8") of cotton hanging out of one end of the bead. Now go over the bead and through the hole until the bead is completely covered with cotton. Leave about 20 cm at the end to match the cotton you have left at the beginning.

Thread three antique glass beads, Mill Hill No. 3028, onto your cotton and take your needle down through the pebble bead for the last time. The three seed beads will sit on the end of the pebble bead. The threads you have left hanging are used to sew the berry onto the beret. Make 12 of these berries in the same way.

12. Thread the two threads of the berry through your No. 9 crewel needle and sew the berry to the centre of the berry stem. Do not have the berry tight against the fabric, but leave it hanging with a 12 mm ($^1/2$") stem.

Bring the needle back to the right side and catch a few threads of the berry at the bottom of the pebble bead. The stem that is hanging can be buttonhole stitched and then finished off at the back. Sew three berries on the end of each berry stem.

*Version 2 – shown on Scarf*

To work the design, you will need a piece of navy woollen dress fabric (that matches colour of beret if you wish), 48 cm x 1.5 m (19" x 59"), plus the materials and threads listed for Version 1.

Transfer the design chart on page 36 onto the wool fabric using a white marker. Now follow instructions for Version 1 above.

To make up the scarf, follow the instructions on page 51.

*Version 3 – shown on Greeting Card*

If you have worked the beret or scarf, you will not have to purchase any threads as you should have enough left over.

REQUIREMENTS
**Materials:**
Woollen fabric, 15 cm x 15 cm (6")
Blue satin ribbon, 25 cm (10") x 5 mm ($^1/4$") wide
Blue braid, enough to go around the opening of the card plus
    a small overlap
No. 18 chenille needles

**Threads:**
Anchor tapestry wool
– Nos 8740, 8738, 8734 and 8880
Charleston No. 108
Kirra yarns Mohair No. 434
Wisper 80% Kid mohair 20% Nylon No W93
DMC Perle 3 No. 930
DMC Medici No. 8308

Increase at 120%
**Lavender and Bullion Roses –
Greeting Card**

Outline the opening in the card on the woollen fabric using a white marking pencil. Trace the design chart with the white marker. Now follow steps 2, 3, 4, 7, 8, 9 and 10 in the instructions for Version 1 above.

To make up the greeting card, refer to the instructions on page 49, steps 1, 2 and 3 only. Then glue the braid around the opening on the front of the card. Where the braid joins, tie a small bow out of your satin ribbon and glue the bow over the join.

### BULLION ROSE BOUQUET

*Version 1 – shown on Jewellery Box Lid*

REQUIREMENTS
**Materials:**
Woollen dress fabric, 2 pieces each 25 cm x 25 cm (10")
Wooden jewellery box with 11 cm (4 1/4") square opening for embroidery (jewellery boxes are available through Delwood Designs – see page 135 for more details)
No. 20 chenille needles
No. 10 crewel needles
Mill Hill antique glass beads No. 03003

**Threads:**
Appletons crewel wool
– Nos 226, 223, 222 and 333
DMC stranded cotton No. 3778
Anchor stranded cotton No. 856

**Stitches used:**
Bullion stitch, fly stitch, straight stitch, whipped chain stitch, satin stitch, lazy daisy stitch, colonial knots and continuous fly stitch.

To embroider lid:

1.  Transfer the design chart on page 39 with a water soluble pen to one of the pieces of fabric (see page 3).

2.  With a No. 20 chenille needle, embroider the bullion roses with 6 twists:
    1st row – Appletons crewel wool No. 226.
    2nd row – Appletons crewel wool No. 223.
    3rd row – Appletons crewel wool No. 222.

3.  Embroider the rose leaves using Appletons crewel wool No. 333.

4.  Embroider the rose buds:
    1st row – Appletons crewel wool No. 226.
    2nd row – Appletons crewel wool No. 222.
    3rd row – Appletons crewel wool No. 333.

5.  Chain stitch the bow in Appletons crewel wool No. 223 and whip the chain in DMC stranded cotton No. 3778.

6.  Satin stitch the knot of the bow next using three strands of DMC stranded cotton No. 3778.

7.  Embroider the straight stitch stems above and below the bow using one strand of Anchor stranded cotton No. 856.

8.  Embroider the lazy daisy flowers using Appletons crewel wool No. 222. Work one colonial knot in Appletons crewel wool No. 223 for the centres of the lazy daisy flowers.

9.  Embroider the continuous fly stitch fern that goes with the lazy daisy using one strand of Anchor stranded cotton No. 856.

10. Embroider the fine stems using one strand of Anchor stranded cotton No. 856. These stems consist of one fly stitch with a stem and one straight stitch in the centre.

11. Attach a Mill Hill glass seed bead No. 03003 to the tip of each fine stem. Sew on each bead separately. Each set of fine stems has three sets of three beads, nine beads in total.

Jewellery Box Lid – *actual size*

Jewellery Box Base and Greeting Card – *actual size*

Bullion Rose Bouquet

To embroider inside base:

1.  Transfer the design above to the other piece of fabric with a water soluble pen.

2.  Follow steps 2 to 4 of the instructions for embroidering the lid.

3. Embroider the lazy daisy flower next using Appletons crewel wool No. 222. The centre of the lazy daisy flower is worked in one colonial knot using Appletons crewel wool No. 223.

4. Embroider the continuous fly stitch fern that goes with the lazy daisy next using one strand of Anchor stranded cotton No. 856.

5. Follow steps 10 and 11 of the instructions for embroidering the lid.

If you are purchasing one of my jewellery boxes, you will receive full instructions on how to assemble your embroidery into the jewellery box. If you are not confident of assembling your embroidery, send it to a good embroidery framer.

*Version 2 – shown on Greeting Card*

If you wish to apply the design to a card, you will need a piece of wool blanketing 15 cm x 15 cm (6"), plus the needles, beads and threads listed for Version 1. If you have made the jewellery box, you will not have to purchase any threads or beads. You will have enough left over.

I recommend you follow the design used on the inside base of the jewellery box (page 39). Trace the design onto the fabric with a water soluble pen. Now follow the instructions above.

To make up the greeting card, refer to the instructions given on page 49.

### JEWELLERY DESIGNS

I suggest you work the embroidery for all the jewellery on the one piece of fabric and then cut each piece out as you make it up. Make sure you leave enough space between each item. Please check the flower and stitch guides at all times.

*Version 1 – Pendant*

REQUIREMENTS
**Materials:**
Cream wool crepe fabric, 15 cm x 15 cm (6")
Appletons crewel wool
– Nos 143, 142, 751 and 292
No. 20 chenille needles

**Stitches used:**
Bullion stitch, straight stitch and fly stitch.

1. Transfer the design chart with a water soluble pen to the fabric (see page 3). It is a good idea to trace the opening of the pendant as well.

actual size
**Pendant and Greeting Card**

2. Embroider the small bullion rose (see page 6). In this bullion rose, use 6 twists only.
   1st row – Appletons crewel wool No. 143.
   2nd row – Appletons crewel wool No. 142.
   3rd row – Appletons crewel wool No. 751.

3. Embroider the small fly stitch rose leaves next using Appletons crewel wool No. 292.

4. Embroider the small bullion rose buds. Work in the same way as the large bullion buds, only use less twists:
   1st row – one bullion stitch only, 4 twists, Appletons crewel wool No. 143.
   2nd row – one bullion each side of centre bullion, 4 twists, Appletons crewel wool No. 751.
   3rd row – one fly stitch around the bud and take the stem back to the rose, Appletons crewel wool No. 292.

   Embroider two small straight stitches on the top of the rose bud with the same wool.

   To make up the pendant, refer to page 52.

*Version 2 – Brooch*

There is no need to transfer this embroidery as there is only one rose.

1. Embroider the tiny bullion rose (see page 6). In this rose use 4 twists only, and check the flower guide for petal placement.
   1st row – Appletons crewel wool No. 143.
   2nd row – Appletons crewel wool No. 142.
   3rd row – Appletons crewel wool No. 751.

2. Embroider the small fly stitch rose leaves using Appletons crewel wool No. 292.

   To make up the brooch, refer to page 52.

*Version 3 – Earrings*

There is no need to transfer this embroidery as there is only one rose. Keep the rose very small.

   To work the design, follow step 1 of the instructions for Version 2 above. Then, using Appletons crewel wool No. 292, embroider a fly stitch around the rose and make a very small stem.

   Embroider the other earring in the same way.

   To make up the earrings, refer to page 52.

If you wish to embroider a greeting card to go with the jewellery, you will not have to buy any threads and you will also have enough fabric. I would suggest you use the pendant design.

   To make up the greeting card, refer to the instructions given on page 49.

**Brooch** – actual size

**Earrings** – actual size

# CHAPTER 6

# SEWING PROJECTS

You can apply the designs in Chapter 5 to the following sewing projects.

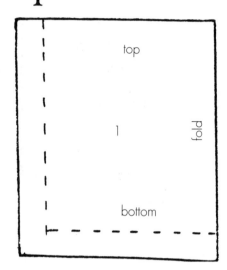

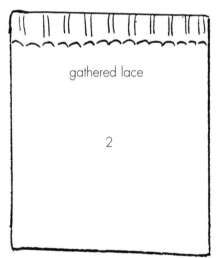

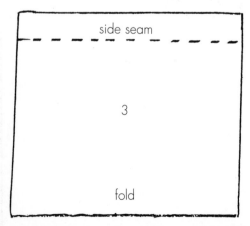

## LINGERIE BAG

REQUIREMENTS
Wool blanketing, 60 cm x 38 cm (23 $^3$/4" x 15")
Cotton fabric, 60 cm x 38 cm, to line lingerie bag
Cream lace, 1.5 m (59") x 6.5 cm (2 $^1$/2") wide, or 60 cm of pregathered lace, or 55 cm (21 $^3$/4") of straight lace 5 cm (2") wide
Cream double-sided satin ribbon, 2 m (78") x 10 mm ($^3$/8") wide

Cut out the wool blanketing and the cotton fabric using the pattern provided on page 44. Complete the embroidery on the wool fabric.

1. On the wool fabric only, machine four buttonholes where the markings are on the pattern, and then cut them. The buttonholes are 12 mm ($^1$/2") in length.

2. With right sides of the wool fabric together, allowing 5 mm ($^1$/4") seams, machine the side seam and the bottom edge of the bag (diag. 1). Turn the bag to the right side.

3. Gather the lace to fit the top of the bag. Sew two rows of large machine stitches, about 5 mm ($^1$/4") apart, along the top edge of the lace. Draw the threads up to make the lace fit the top of the bag, and pin in place. If you are using pregathered lace, or the straight lace (for the Australian Wildflowers lingerie bag), pin the lace around the top of the bag, with the scalloped edge of the lace facing down. Sew the lace 5 mm down from the top edge (diag. 2).

4. Take the piece of cotton fabric, which has been cut the same size as the woollen fabric, and sew the side seam only with a 5 mm ($^1$/4") seam. Leave the bottom edge of the cotton bag open (diag. 3).

5. Turn the cotton fabric to the wrong side and slip the cotton fabric over the top of the woollen bag. The right sides should be facing each other.

6. Pin the top edge of the woollen bag to the top edge of the cotton fabric bag. Place the lace edging between the cotton bag and the woollen bag. Machine these top edges together with 5 mm ($^1$/4") seams.

7. Turn the woollen bag to the right side and fold the cotton fabric bag inside the woollen bag. The cotton fabric forms the lining of the woollen bag. The lace will now stand out of the top of the bag (diag. 4).

8. Mark a pin line around the top of the bag, through both cotton and woollen bags, 3 cm (1 1/4") down from the fabric edge, not the lace edge. Machine along the pin line you have just marked. Mark another pin line about 2 cm (3/4") down from the previous stitching, and machine along this line (diag. 5). You have just made the casing for the ribbon draw strings.

9. Turn the cotton bag out and turn the raw edges of the cotton bag in 2.5 cm (1"). Pin to hold in place. Machine along the bottom edge.

10. Cut the double-sided satin ribbon into two pieces. Using a safety pin, thread one piece of ribbon through the buttonhole, right around the bag through the casing, and out of the buttonhole next to where you started. Tie both ends of the ribbon together in a knot.

11. Thread the other piece of ribbon through the opposite buttonhole and out at the buttonhole next to where you started. Tie both ends of the ribbon together in a knot, and draw the ribbons up to close the bag (diag. 6).

4

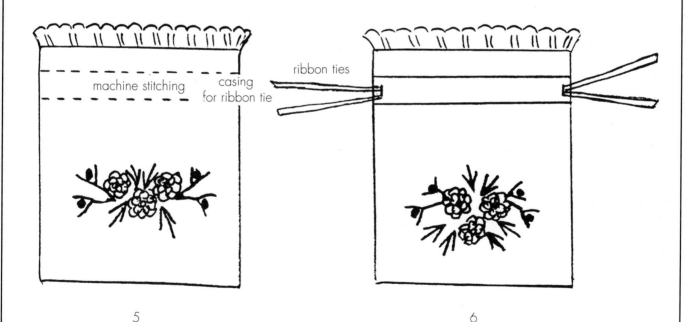

5

6

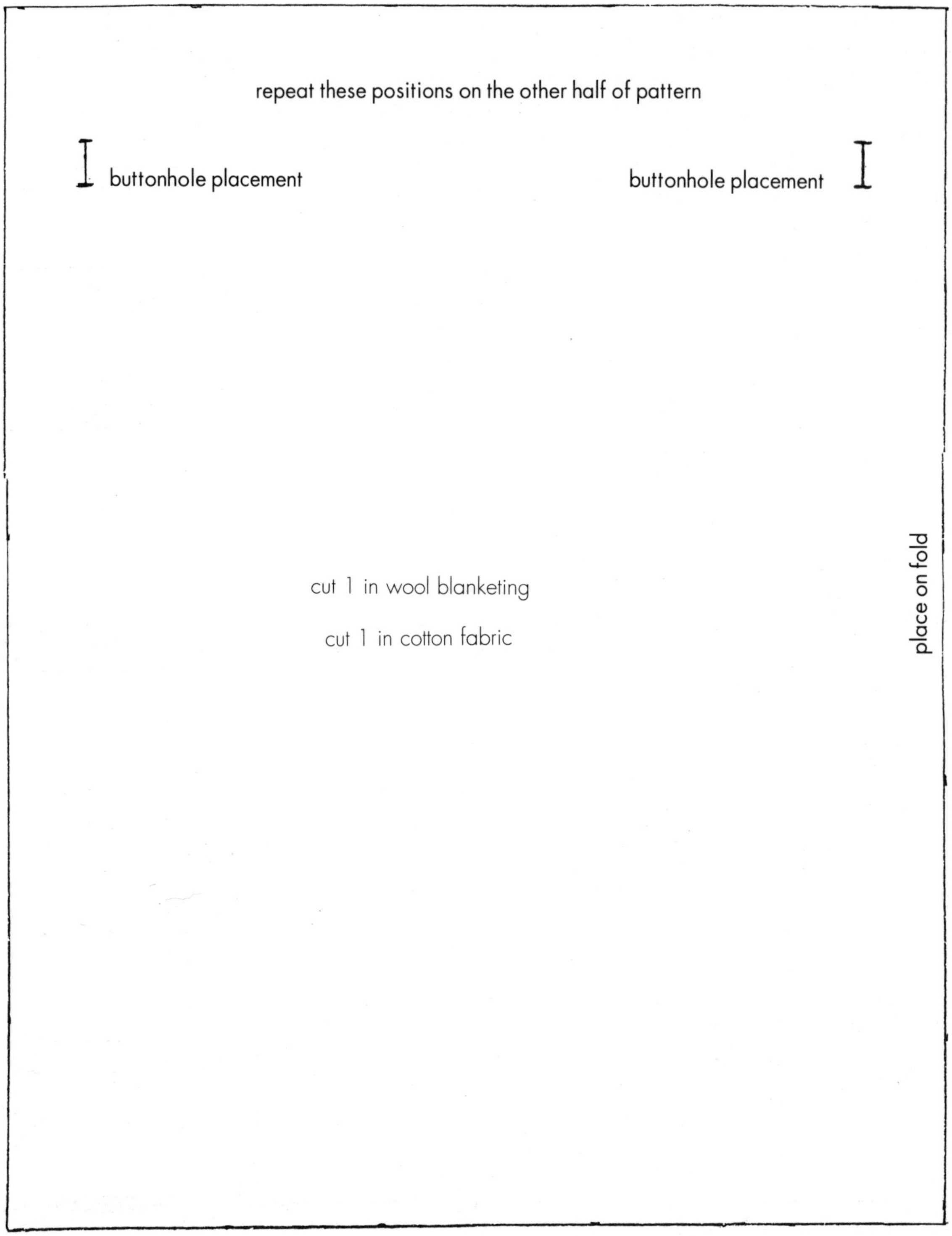

repeat these positions on the other half of pattern

I buttonhole placement

buttonhole placement I

cut 1 in wool blanketing

cut 1 in cotton fabric

place on fold

Increase at 200%

Pattern for lingerie bag

## WOODEN COATHANGER COVER

REQUIREMENTS
Wool blanketing, 56 cm x 38 cm (22" x 15")
Wadding, 25 cm (10") length
Wooden coathanger
Plastic tubing, 15 cm (6") long, or satin fabric for bias binding
    hook cover
No. 9 crewel needle
Cream lace, 2 m (78") x 6.5 cm (2 1/2") wide, or 130 cm (51")
    of pregathered lace
Cream double-sided satin ribbon, 40 cm (15 3/4") x 10 mm
    (3/8")wide

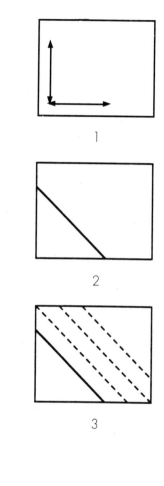

Cut two pieces of wool blanketing as per pattern on page 47 for the coathanger. The seam allowance has been added to the pattern. Now complete the embroidery.

1. Cut the wadding into strips 7.5 cm (3") wide, and bind the wooden coathanger with the wadding. This forms the padding for the coathanger. It is a good idea to hand sew the wadding ends so that they do not unravel. Leave the hook in the hanger while you are binding as it is very hard to replace the hook once the wadding is on the hanger.

2. Push the plastic tubing over the hook of the hanger. Satin bias binding can be used for the hook as well but it is not practical as it wears badly. However, if you do wish to cover the hook with bias binding, here's how it's done:

    Find the straight of the satin fabric (diag. 1), and then measure an equal distance from the corner of the fabric up and across the fabric. Mark these two points, and then join them – the line indicates the bias of the fabric (diag. 2).

    Using this line as a guide, cut a bias strip 2.5 cm (1") in width and long enough to cover the hook of the hanger, plus small turnings (diag. 3).

    Fold the fabric over lengthwise, with the rights sides facing and the raw edges matching. Machine a line of stitching 5 mm (1/4") from the fold (diag. 4). Do not trim the seam.

    Cut the end of the tubing as in diagram 5. Thread a needle with a strong sewing thread, and secure the thread to the point of the tubing (diag. 6). (Do not secure it too close to the edge or the fabric will fray.) Leading with the eye of the needle, thread the needle through the tube. When you reach the other end, pull on the thread and the fabric will turn to the right side (diag. 7).

    Thread the tubing over the hook of the hanger, turn the raw end in and hand sew. Hand sew the tubing also at the hook base.

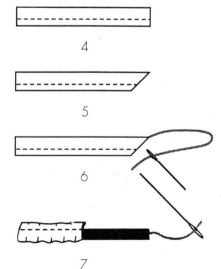

3. Overlock or oversew by hand both bottom edges of both pieces of wool blanketing.

4. Sew the lace to the bottom edges of the fabric. To gather the lace yourself, sew two rows of large machine stitches along the top edge of the lace about 5 mm ($^{1}/4$") apart. Draw the threads up to make the lace fit the bottom edge of the fabric. Gather each piece of lace separately. When you have the lace gathered to size, pin and then sew the lace to the right side of the fabric, either by machine or by hand (diag. 8).

5. With the right sides facing, sew the top edge of the hanger pieces together with a 5 mm ($^{1}/4$") seam allowance. Leave a 12 mm ($^{1}/2$") opening in the centre so that the hook of the hanger can go through (diag. 9). Hand sew the seam allowance back around the hook opening. Turn the fabric to the right side and slip it over the prepared padded coat hanger.

6. Sew both bottom edges of the fabric together by hand. Tie a ribbon bow around the hook of the hanger.

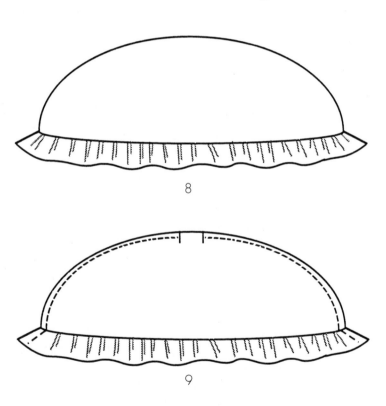

8

9

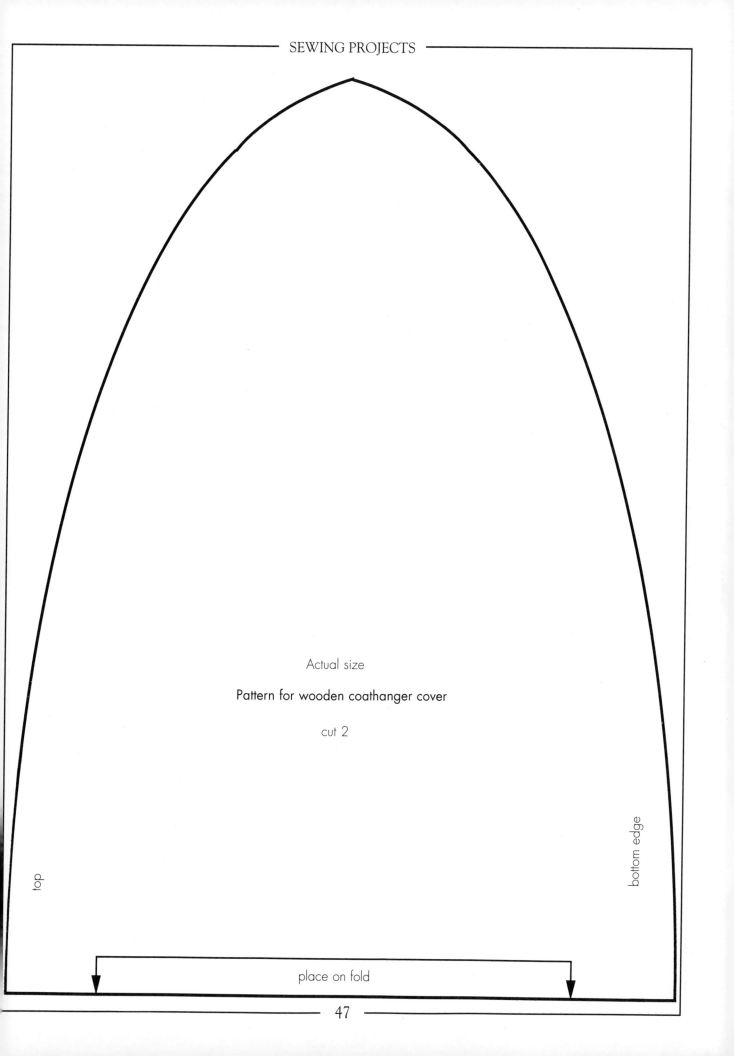

Actual size

Pattern for wooden coathanger cover

cut 2

top

bottom edge

place on fold

## WIRE COATHANGER COVER

REQUIREMENTS
Wool blanketing, 45 cm x 50 cm (17 $^3$/4" x 19 $^3$/4")
Wadding, 45 cm x 50 cm (17 $^3$/4" x 19 $^3$/4")
Wire coathanger
No. 9 crewel needle
Cream sewing cotton
Plastic tubing, 15 cm (6") long, or satin fabric for bias binding
    hook cover
Cream cotton lace, 1 m (39") x 5 cm (2") wide
Cream double-sided satin ribbon, 40 cm (15 $^3$/4") x 10 mm
    ($^3$/8") wide

Cut two pieces of wool blanketing and two pieces of wadding as per wire coathanger pattern below. Now complete the embroidery.

1. Place the wire coathanger between the two pieces of wadding and pin. With the crewel needle threaded with cream double sewing thread, oversew the pieces of wadding together, around all sides. The wire coathanger is now secured inside the wadding.

2. Now follow steps 2 to 6 of the instructions for covering a wooden coathanger, pages 45 to 46.

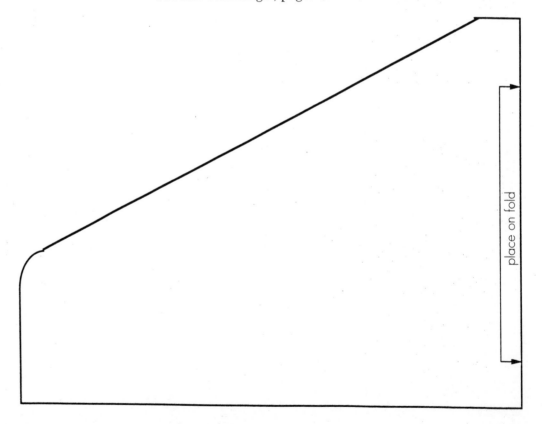

place on fold

Increase at 200%

Pattern for wire coathanger cover

WOOL ROSE BOUQUET WITH CREAM BOW ON LINGERIE BAG AND COATHANGER COVER

ABOVE: WOOL ROSES AND BUTTONHOLE FLOWERS ON DOORSTOP

ARRAY OF GREETING CARDS

WOOL-EMBROIDERED HEART ON LINGERIE BAG AND COATHANGER COVER

AUSTRALIAN WILDFLOWERS ON LINGERIE BAG AND COATHANGER COVER

## GREETING CARD

REQUIREMENTS
Card, especially for embroidery
Wadding, the same size as the embroidered wool blanketing
Craft glue
Embroidered wool blanketing, 12 cm x 16 cm (4 3/4" x 6 1/4")
Pregathered lace, the length of the opening in the card plus a
    small amount for turnings
Cream double-sided satin ribbon, 25 cm (10") x 5 mm (1/4")
    wide

1. Glue the piece of wadding to the flat side of the card (diag.
   1, page 50). This will give the embroidery a padded look.

2. Place the embroidered wool blanketing over the opening on
   the wrong side of the card. You will have to trim some of the
   fabric away. When it is cut to size, glue the embroidered
   fabric to the inside of the card (diag. 2, page 50). The
   embroidery will be facing the front of the card.

3. When the above is dry, glue the embroidered front of the
   card to the back of the card with the wadding on it. Hold
   firmly until the glue is dry. Clothes pegs are good to use as
   clamps while the glue is drying.

4. Take the pregathered lace and glue the lace around the
   opening on the front of the card. Tie a small bow out of the
   ribbon and glue over the join in the lace.

## DOOR STOP

REQUIREMENTS
Circle of embroidered wool blanketing, 35 cm (13 3/4") in diameter
Strong sewing thread
No. 9 crewel needle
Toy filling
Empty tin, 750 g (26 oz) in size
Wadding, enough to cover the tin
Rocks or sand, to fill tin
Circle of green velvet, 48 cm (19") in diameter
Braid to match velvet, 1 m (39") length

1. With a strong sewing thread doubled, work a small running
   stitch around the embroidered circle about 12 mm (1/2") in
   from the edge. You may start with a knot in your thread but
   you should also do two or three overstitches to hold the
   thread firm. This thread is going to be used to gather this
   edge in and has to be able to withstand a great deal of strain.
   Do not end off this thread or cut off the needle.

2. Draw up the gathering thread until you have a very tight
   circle, secure with a couple of overstitches and then finish
   off. Do not gather up the circle completely, as it has to be
   stuffed with toy filling.

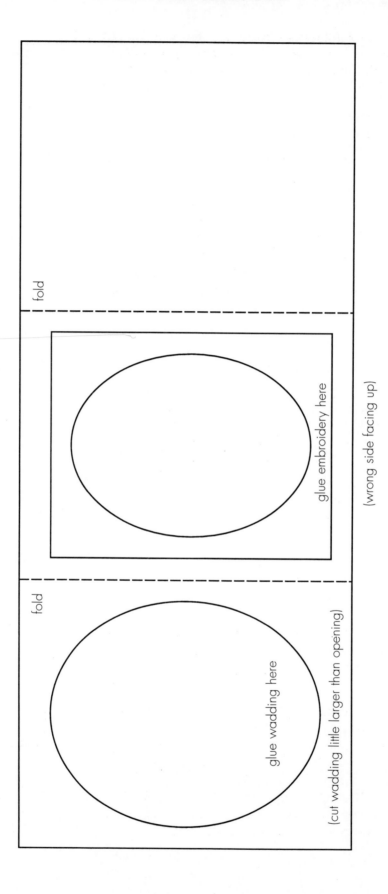

fold

glue embroidery here

(wrong side facing up)

fold

glue wadding here

(cut wadding little larger than opening)

Pattern for greeting card

3. Start stuffing the toy filling into the circle. You will end up with a giant mushroom shape. Use the end of a wooden spoon to push the filling firmly into the mushroom. (The firmer the better.)

4. Cover the tin with wadding, to give the base a padded look. Glue the wadding to the tin with craft glue.

5. Fill the tin with rocks or sand. Cover the top of the tin with wadding to keep the rocks or sand in place.

6. Take the chenille needle and strong sewing thread, doubled, and work a small running stitch around the circle of velvet, about 12 mm ($^1/2$") in from the edge. You will need a fairly long thread as it is a large circle. Start with a knot in the thread but also do two or three overstitches to hold the thread firm. It is going to be used to gather the edge and will have to withstand a great deal of strain.

7. Place the tin inside the circle and gather in the velvet tightly. The velvet will come up over the top of the tin. Secure the thread off with a couple of overstitches.

8. With the chenille needle and strong thread matching the velvet, ladder stitch the wool mushroom to the velvet-covered base and finish off securely.

9. Glue braid around the join of the mushroom, and also to the lower edge of the base.

## SCARF

REQUIREMENTS
Embroidered navy woollen dress fabric, 48 cm x 1.5 m
   (19" x 59")
No. 9 crewel needle
Navy sewing cotton

1. Fold your embroidery in half lengthwise, right sides facing, and pin together. Machine across the ends and along the side. Make sure you leave an opening in the centre of the long side 10 cm (4") in length.

2. Turn the scarf to the right side through the opening you have left.

3. With the navy sewing thread and No. 9 crewel needle, ladder stitch the opening closed. Iron the scarf when you have finished (see page 3 for instructions on ironing embroidery).

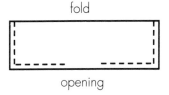

fold

opening

## JEWELLERY PIECES

REQUIREMENTS
Small piece of template plastic
Wadding (thin)
Craft glue
Embroidered wool crepe fabric
Fray Stopper
No. 9 crewel needle
Cream sewing thread
Oval jewellery mount for each of the following:
– Pendant, 4 cm (1 3/8") in length
– Brooch, 2 cm (3/4") in length
– Earrings, 12 mm (1/2") in length
Small piece of felt

*Note:* The jewellery mounts shown in the colour section are from Ireland Needle Craft in Melbourne (phone: (03) 702 3222).

*Pendant* _____

1. Cut a piece of template plastic just slightly smaller than the opening in the pendant. Glue a small piece of wadding on one side of the plastic.

2. Cut out the embroidered fabric, allowing 5 mm (1/4") more than the opening in the pendant. Fray Stopper around the raw edge.

3. Using a No. 9 crewel needle and cream sewing thread, sew a running stitch around the outside edge about 3 mm (1/8") in from the edge. Knot the thread to start with, and take two or three overstitches to hold the knot firm. Leave the thread in the needle. Place the template plastic shape with the wadding on it face down on the wrong side of the embroidery. Gather the thread in and the fabric will come up over the plastic shape. Finish off the thread when the fabric is firmly in place.

4. Place the embroidery into the jewellery mount. Glue a piece of felt at the back of the embroidery. Fold the small claws over on the back of the jewellery mount.

*Brooch* _____

Assemble the brooch in the same manner as the pendant. However, you will not have to glue any felt to the back of your work. Glue the embroidery directly into the mount once you have secured it on your template plastic shape. Fold the mount edges over now.

*Earrings* _____

Assemble your earrings in the same manner as the brooch.

# Chapter 7

# MAJOR PROJECTS

Where more than one skein is required of any particular colour, I have indicated the amount beside the colour number.

Check the flower and stitch guides at all times. Always check whether the embroidery design charts have to be enlarged on a photocopier.

### BOUQUET OF CREAM CAMELLIAS

The bullion stitch camellias are quite difficult to work, and so both versions of this design require some degree of embroidery experience.

*Knee Rug*

REQUIREMENTS
**Materials:**
Wool blanketing, 80 cm x 110 cm (31 $^1/2$" x 43 $^1/4$")
Pure silk fabric or cotton, 125 cm (49 $^1/4$") for the blanket
    backing
Cream lace, 8 m (8 $^1/2$ yds) x 5 cm (2") wide
Cream sewing thread
Mill Hill glass pebble beads No. 05147
Cream pearl beads
No. 18 chenille needles
Doll needles, 10 cm (4") long
Nos 9 and 10 crewel needles

**Threads:**
DMC Perle 5
– Nos 739 and 712
Appletons tapestry wool No. 992 (10 skeins)
Patina 100% Rayon thread No. PA01
DMC Perle 3 No. 712
Kirra yarns Mohair No. 330
DMC stranded cotton No. 712

*Note:* I backed my blanket with pure silk, but you can use cotton backing if you prefer.

In this project I have used a range of needle sizes. Please read carefully for needle changes.

**Stitches used:**
Whipped chain stitch, satin stitch, lazy daisy stitch, straight stitch, colonial knots, continuous fly stitch, bullion stitch, stem stitch and buttonhole stitch.

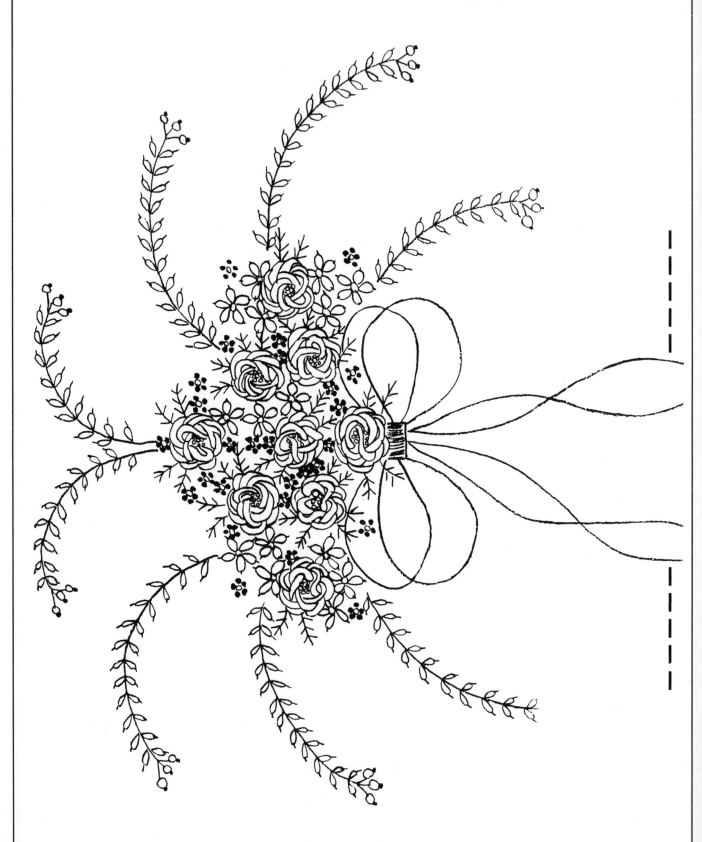

Increase at 200%

Bouquet of Cream Camellias – Knee Rug

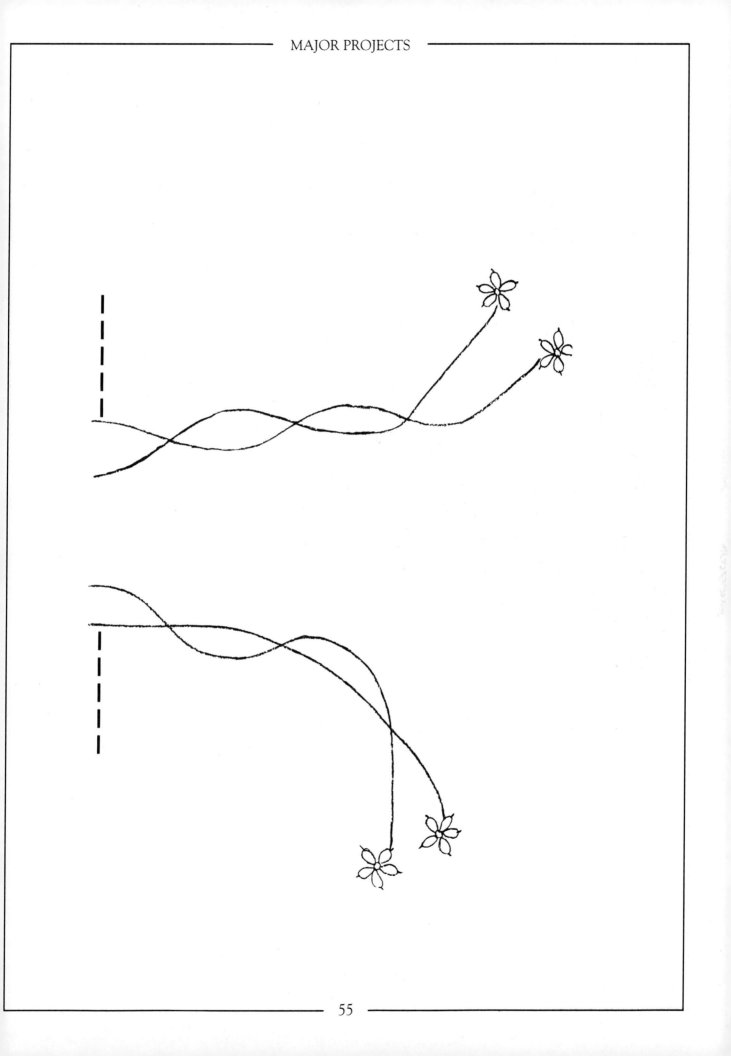

To embroider blanket:

1. Transfer the bow from the design chart on pages 54 and 55 to the wool blanketing (see page 3). Using a No. 18 chenille needle and DMC Perle 5 No. 739, chain stitch the bow first and then whip the chain. It is best to embroider one section of the bow at a time and whip that section straight away.

2. Using a No. 18 chenille needle and DMC Perle 5 No. 739, satin stitch the knot of the bow.

3. Mark the positions of the camellias next, but do not embroider them.

4. Mark and embroider the lazy daisy flowers using Appletons tapestry wool No. 992 and a No. 18 chenille needle.

5. Embroider small straight stitches over the end of the lazy daisy petals with Patina thread No. PA01 and a No. 18 chenille needle. Make sure you start and end this thread off well as it is a rayon thread.

6. With a No. 9 crewel needle and double cream sewing thread, sew the cream pearls in the centre of each lazy daisy flower. End each pearl off separately.

7. Mark the forget-me-nots next. Work the colonial knots using a No. 18 chenille needle:
Petals – Appletons tapestry wool No. 992.
Centres – DMC Perle 3 No. 712.

8. Embroider the continuous fly stitch leaves using a No. 18 chenille needle and Kirra yarns Mohair No. 330.

9. Embroider the bullion camellia flowers next with a doll needle and Appletons tapestry wool No. 992. Make the thread about 64 cm (25") long. These flowers require a large amount of wool because of the many wraps per petal. You might only get two petals out of this 64 cm thread. Check the flower and stitch guides for the number of wraps and the positioning of the petals.

10. Fill the centre of the camellia flowers with colonial knots. Use a No. 18 chenille needle and DMC Perle 3 No. 712.

11. Mark and embroider the berry stems and leaves using a No. 18 chenille needle and DMC Perle 5 No. 712. Stems are embroidered in stem stitch, while the leaves are lazy daisy stitch.

12. Next make the berries. This method was taught to me by Jane Nicholas. Measure out a 127 cm (50") length of DMC stranded cotton No. 712. From the six strands, take one strand at a time and make a berry.

Thread the cotton in a No. 10 crewel needle. Take one of the Mill Hill glass pebble beads and thread the cotton in the needle through the hole in the bead. Leave about 20 cm (8") of thread hanging out of one end of the bead. Go over the bead and through the hole until the bead is completely covered with the cotton. You will use almost all the thread. Leave about 20 cm at the end to match the thread you have left at the beginning.

Thread a pearl on at the end and take the thread down through the hole in the pebble bead for the last time. The threads you have left hanging are used to sew the berry onto the blanket.

Make 24 of these berries in the same manner.

13. Sew three berries on the end of each berry stem. Thread the two threads of the berry through your No. 9 crewel needle and sew the berry to the centre of the berry stem. Do not have the berry tight against the blanket, but leave it hanging with a 12 mm (1/2") stem. Bring the needle back to the right side and catch a few threads of the berry at the bottom of the pebble bead. You now have a small stem and a hanging berry. Buttonhole stitch the hanging stem and then end it off at the back of the blanket. Sew all the berries on in the same way.

To back blanket:

It is a good idea to round the corners of your blanket slightly. It will make it much easier to sew on the lace. You should also wash and iron the backing fabric before using it.

1. Lay the backing fabric down on a table, wrong side up, and pin the wool blanketing with the embroidery facing up onto the backing fabric. Hand tack the backing fabric to the wool blanket 12 mm (1/2") from the edge. Trim away excess backing fabric and overlock the edges, as in the diagram.

2. Divide the outside edge of the blanket into quarters and mark each quarter with a pin.

3. Gather the lace to fit the outside edge of the blanket. I gather my own lace but you can buy pregathered lace. To gather the lace yourself, sew two rows of large machine stitches along the top edge of the lace about 5 mm (1/4") apart. Divide the lace into four and mark each quarter with a pin. Gather the lace to fit the outside edge of the blanket, matching each quarter of the lace and the blanket. By using this method, you will gather the lace evenly all the way around the blanket.

4. Pin the gathered lace around the right side of the blanket about 12 mm (1/2") in from the edge, and then machine the lace on. If you are using pregathered lace, pin the lace around the edge and machine the lace on.

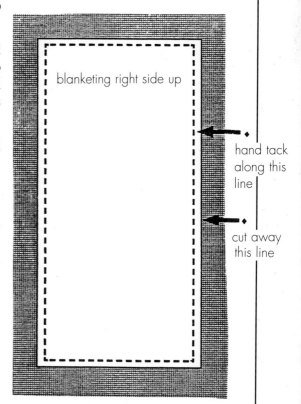

blanketing right side up

hand tack along this line

cut away this line

backing fabric wrong side up

5. Once you have sewn on the lace, you can remove the tacking thread if it is showing.

6. Secure the backing fabric to the blanketing through a few camellias. With a No. 9 crewel needle and cream sewing thread, catch a few camellias through the backing fabric with a couple of stab stitches. Stab stitching is just a stitch up through the fabric and back down through the fabric. End each stab stitch off securely.

## Cushion

REQUIREMENTS

**Materials:**
Wool blanketing, 51 cm x 51 cm (20")
Cotton fabric or pure silk, 125 cm (49 $^1$/4"), for backing and frill
Cream lace, 5 m (5 $^1$/2 yds), for frill (optional)
Cream zipper, 45 cm (17 $^3$/4") long
Cream sewing thread
Cushion insert, 3.5 cm (1 $^1$/2") larger than the cushion,
    or 55 cm x 55 cm (21 $^3$/4")
Mill Hill glass pebble beads No. 05147
Cream pearl beads
No. 18 chenille needle
Doll needles, 10 cm (4") in length
Nos 9 and 10 crewel needles

**Threads:**
DMC Perle 5
– Nos 739 and 712
Appletons tapestry wool No. 992 (6 skeins)
Patina 100% Rayon thread No. PA01
DMC Perle 3 No. 712
Kirra yarns Mohair No. 330
DMC stranded cotton No. 712

*Note:* I have made the frill on this cushion out of pure silk to match the blanket. You could use cotton or pure silk.

To embroider cushion:

Transfer the bow from the design chart on page 59 to the cushion blanketing (see page 3). Now follow steps 2 to 13 of the instructions for working the design for the knee rug, above. In step 12 make 18 berries instead of 24 berries.

To make up cushion:

It is a good idea to round the corners of the embroidered cushion piece slightly as this will make it easier to sew on the frill. Cut two pieces of cotton fabric, 53.5 cm x 29 cm (21" x 11 $^1$/2"), for the cushion backing.

Increase at 200%

Bouquet of Cream Camellias – Cushion

1. Place the two cotton squares rights sides together and sew down 4.5 cm (1 3/4") from each end of the longest side seam. Leave the middle section open for the 45 cm zipper. (The seam allowance is 2.5 cm, or 1".) Sew the zipper in the opening of the seam.

2. Cut four pieces of cotton or pure silk fabric for the frill, 115 cm x 15 cm ( 45" x 6").

3. Join the four pieces of frilling together to form a circle (12 mm, or 1/2", seams have been allowed).

4. Fold the frill in half along its length and iron a crease in the centre.

5. If you would like to have a lace and silk frill, lay the lace on top of the frill when sewing the gathering threads. Start at a seam and sew two rows of gathering threads, about 5 mm (1/4") apart. Use a long stitch.

6. Mark each quarter of the frill with a pin, and divide the outside edge of the embroidered cushion piece into quarters and mark each quarter with a pin. Gather the frill to fit the outside edge of the embroidered cushion, matching each quarter of the frill to the cushion quarters. This method ensures an evenly gathered frill all the way around.

7. Pin the frill around the outside of the embroidered cushion with the fold of the frill facing towards the centre of the cushion. On each quarter marking of the cushion, place a seam of the frill.

8. Machine the frill onto the embroidered cushion piece about 12 mm (1/2") in from the edge. Remove the pins once you have sewn on the frill.

9. Take the back of the cotton cushion with the zipper in it and unzip the zip about 10 cm (4"). Place the right side of the woollen fabric and the right side of the cotton fabric together, and then pin around the outside.

10. Turn the woollen fabric over so that you can see the stitch line where you have just sewn on the frill. Machine stitch both fabrics together around this stitch line.

11. Putting your hand through the opening left in the zip, open the zip completely. Now pull the cushion to the right side through this opening.

12. Place the cushion cover over the cushion insert.

*Greeting Card*

For the card embroidery, you will need the same threads as for the knee rug above (but only 1 skein of Appletons tapestry wool No. 992), plus a piece of wool blanketing, 18 cm x 15 cm (7" x 6").

On the piece of wool blanketing, draw the outline of the opening in the card with a water soluble pen. To work the embroidery, first transfer the bow on the design chart below to the fabric. Then follow steps 2 to 13 of the instructions for working the design for the knee rug, page 56. You will only need to make eight berries (two berries per stem).

To make up the greeting card, refer to the instructions given on page 49.

*actual size*

**Bouquet of Cream Camellias – Greeting Card**

## CRAZY WOOL EMBROIDERY

*Sewing Basket Lid*_____

This design is an enjoyable one to embroider, because of the variety of flowers and stitches included.

REQUIREMENTS
### Materials:
Wool blanketing, 53.5 cm x 43 cm (21" x 17")

Strong rectangular cane basket, approximately 48 cm x 38 cm (19" x 15")

Cotton print fabric, 2 m (78") x 115 cm (45") wide

Cream cotton lace, 5 m (5 $^1/_2$ yds) x 3.5 cm (1 $^1/_4$") wide

Cream bias binding, 3 m (3 $^1/_4$ yds) x 12 mm ($^1/_2$") wide

Elastic, 1.3 m (52 $^1/_2$") x 5 mm ($^1/_4$") wide

4 buttons, 12 mm ($^1/_2$") in diameter

Cream zip, 30 cm (12") long

Cream double-sided satin ribbon, 4 m (4 $^1/_3$ yds) x 2.5 cm (1") wide

Template plastic (available from patchwork shops), 2 sheets will be enough

Cream sewing thread

No. 9 crewel needles

No. 18 chenille needles

Diamante bead for spider, 4 mm ($^3/_{16}$") in diameter

### Threads:
DMC Perle 5
– Nos 931, 932, 501 and 738

Gold Rush 62% Metalised, 38% Nylon No. X2

DMC Perle 3
– Nos 930 and 3045 (2 skeins)

Appletons crewel wool
– Nos 323, 295, 643 and 693

DMC stranded cotton
– Nos 310, 729 and 931

Ribbon Floss No. 142 F-21

Appletons tapestry wool
– Nos 841 (2 skeins), 694, 644 and 692

Anchor tapestry wool
– Nos 8838, 8836, 8832 and 9178 (2 skeins)

*Note:* In this project I used a No.18 chenille needle throughout, even when working with fine wools. The only time I used a No. 9 crewel needle was to sew on the diamante. If you find it uncomfortable using a No. 18 needle, change to a smaller needle.

### Stitches used:
Continuous fly stitch, chain stitch, back stitch, lazy daisy stitch, feather stitch, whipped chain stitch, colonial knots, buttonhole stitch, fly stitch, straight stitch, pistil stitch, stem stitch and bullion stitch.

To work section divider lines:

Use a water soluble pen to mark the section dividers on the piece of wool blanketing. It is important to do this first, otherwise you may make one section too big, and the design will not fit onto the blanketing, which has been cut to the size of the lid of the sewing basket. Embroider each section divider line first before embroidering any flowers.

1.  Working in continuous fly stitch, embroider Divider Line 1 first with DMC Perle 5 No. 931.

2.  Embroider Divider Line 2 next with Gold Rush No. X2 and working in chain stitch.

3.  Embroider Divider Line 3 with DMC Perle 5 No. 932. Work a line of back stitches first and then come back and work a lazy daisy stitch either side of each back stitch.

4.  Embroider Divider Line 4 with DMC Perle 5 No. 738 in feather stitch.

5.  Embroider Divider Line 5 with DMC Perle 5 No. 501 and whipped chain stitch.

6.  Embroider Divider Line 6 with Gold Rush No. X2 and continuous fly stitch.

7.  Embroider Divider Line 7 with DMC Perle 5 No. 501. Work a line of back stitch first and then come back and work a lazy daisy either side of each back stitch.

8.  Embroider Divider Line 8 with Gold Rush No. X2 and continuous fly stitch.

9.  Embroider Divider Line 9 with DMC Perle 5 No. 738. Feather stitch first and then come back and embroider a colonial knot on each spoke of the feather stitch.

10. Embroider Divider Line 10 with DMC Perle 5 No. 501 and whipped chain stitch.

11. Embroider Divider Line 11 with DMC Perle 5 No. 932 and feather stitch.

12. Embroider Divider Line 12 with DMC Perle 5 No. 931. Work a continuous fly stitch first and then embroider a colonial knot on the end of each fly stitch.

13. Embroider Divider Line 13 next with DMC Perle 5 No. 501. Feather stitch first and then come back and embroider a colonial knot on each spoke of the feather stitch.

14. Embroider Divider Line 14 with Gold Rush No. X2 and chain stitch.

15. Embroider Divider Line 15 with DMC Perle 5 No. 738. Work a line of back stitches first and then come back and work a lazy daisy either side of each back stitch.

16. Embroider Divider Line 16 with DMC Perle 5 No. 932. Work a continuous fly stitch first and then embroider a colonial knot on the end of each fly stitch.

17. Embroider Divider Line 17 with DMC Perle 5 No. 501 and feather stitch.

18. Embroider Divider Line 18 next with DMC Perle 5 No. 931. Work a line of back stitches first and then come back and work a lazy daisy either side of each back stitch.

19. Finally, embroider Divider Line 19 with DMC Perle 5 No. 738 and continuous fly stitch.

To embroider flowers in each section:

I suggest you transfer one section of the design at a time, embroider that section and then proceed to transferring and embroidering the next. Time and patience are required to get your work just right.

1. *Section 1* Embroider with buttonhole flowers using Appletons crewel wool No. 323. Embroider the buds and knots with DMC stranded cotton No. 931, using 6 strands. Embroider the leaves and stems next with Appletons crewel wool No. 295.

2. *Section 2* Embroider the spider's web in back stitch with Gold Rush No. X2. Sew the diamante on with a No. 9 crewel needle and cream sewing thread. Embroider the spider's legs next using two strands of DMC stranded cotton No. 310 and straight stitches. The feelers are one pistil stitch and the eyes are colonial knots using two strands of DMC stranded cotton No. 310.

3. *Section 3* Embroider the fern first with Appletons crewel wool No. 295 and continuous fly stitch. Embroider a colonial knot on each fly stitch with DMC stranded cotton No. 729, using 6 strands.

4. *Section 4* Embroider the flowers first in pistil stitch with DMC Perle 5 No. 931. The leaves are next in Appletons crewel wool No. 295 and fly stitch. The flower centres consist of four colonial knots in Ribbon Floss No. 142 F-21.

5. *Section 5* Embroider the lazy daisy flowers first using Appletons tapestry wool No. 841. Tip the flowers next with a fly stitch using Appletons crewel wool No. 693. Then embroider one colonial knot for each flower centre using Appletons tapestry wool No. 694. Embroider the stems with a back stitch and Appletons crewel wool No. 643, then the leaves in the same wool. Embroider a lazy daisy either side of the back stitch plus one at the end.

6. *Section 6* Embroider the stems first using stem stitch and Appletons crewel wool No. 295.

Embroider the large bullion roses next, using 11 wraps for the bullions:

1st row – Anchor tapestry wool No. 8838.

2nd row – Anchor tapestry wool No. 8836.

3rd row – Anchor tapestry wool No. 8832.

Embroider the bullion buds. The centre bullion has 12 wraps using DMC Perle 3 No. 930. The two bullions either side of the centre are in the same thread but they have 10 wraps only.

Embroider the straight stitches at the top of the bullion rose buds using Appletons crewel wool No. 295. Fly stitch around the buds back to the stem using the same wool.

Embroider the wool rose leaves using Anchor tapestry wool No. 9178.

7. *Section 7* Embroider the wool roses:

1st row – Appletons tapestry wool No. 694.

2nd row – Appletons tapestry wool No. 692.

3rd row – Appletons tapestry wool No. 841.

Embroider the wool rose leaves with Appletons tapestry wool No. 644.

Embroider the wool rose buds next:

1st row – Appletons tapestry wool No. 694.

2nd row – Appletons tapestry wool No. 841.

3rd row – Appletons tapestry wool No. 644.

Embroider the fern in continuous fly stitch using Appletons crewel wool No. 693. Embroider one colonial knot on each fly stitch using DMC stranded cotton No. 729.

8. *Section 8* Embroider the wool roses first:

1st row – Anchor tapestry wool No. 8838.

2nd row – Anchor tapestry wool No. 8836.

3rd row – Anchor tapestry wool No. 8832.

Embroider the wool rose buds next:

1st row Anchor tapestry wool No. 8838.

2nd row Anchor tapestry wool No. 8832.

3rd row Anchor tapestry wool No. 9178.

Embroider the lazy daisy flowers next using Ribbon Floss No. 142 F-21. The colonial knot flower centres are worked in Ribbon Floss as well.

9. *Section 9* Embroider the stems first using stem stitch and Appletons crewel wool No. 643.

Embroider the large bullion rose next, using 11 wraps for the bullion stitch:

1st row – Appletons tapestry wool No. 694.

2nd row – Appletons tapestry wool No. 692.

3rd row – Appletons tapestry wool No. 841.

Embroider the bullion buds. The centre bullion has 12 wraps using DMC Perle 3 No. 3045. The two bullions

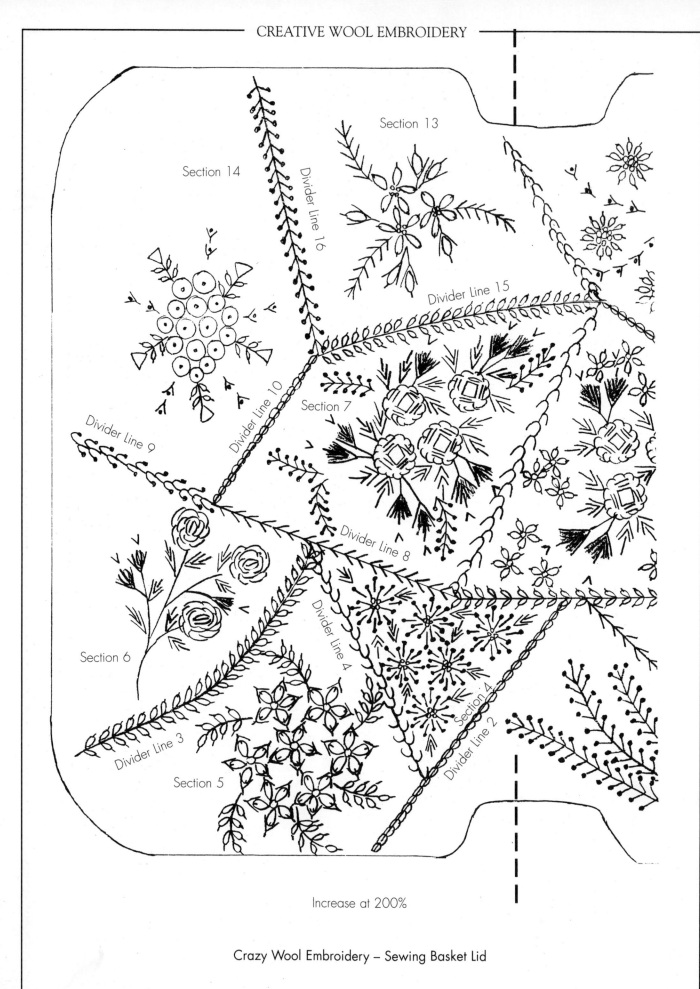

Section 13

Section 14

Divider Line 16

Divider Line 15

Divider Line 10

Divider Line 9

Section 7

Divider Line 8

Divider Line 4

Section 6

Section 4

Divider Line 2

Divider Line 3

Section 5

Increase at 200%

Crazy Wool Embroidery – Sewing Basket Lid

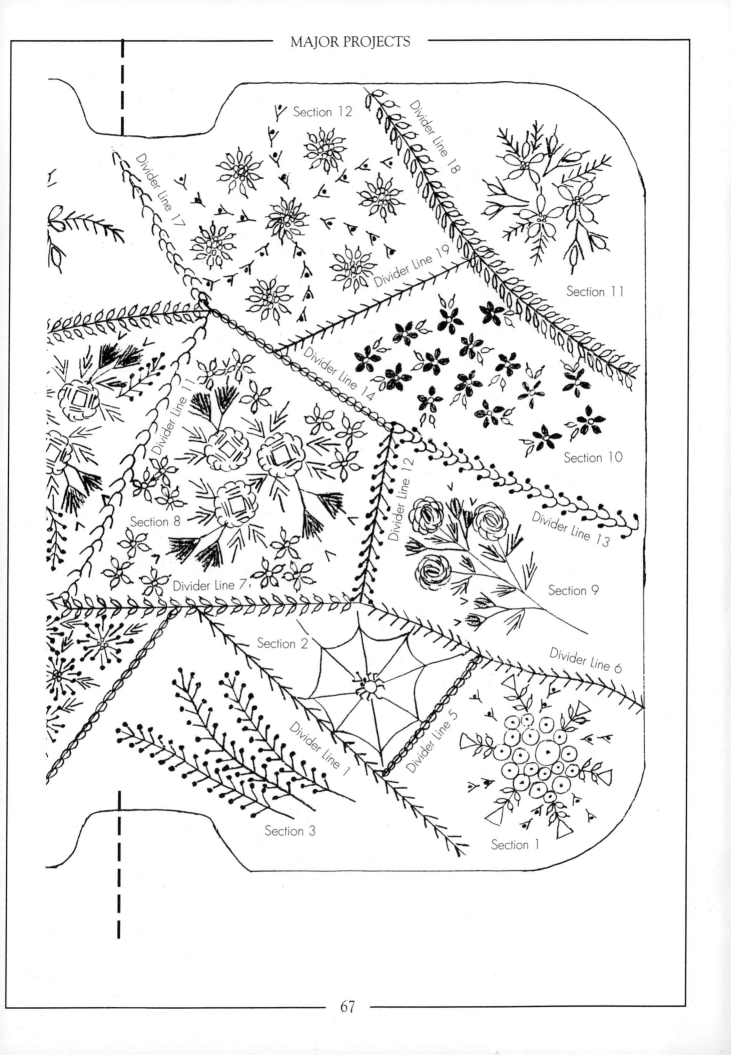

either side of the centre are in the same thread but they have 10 wraps only.

Embroider the straight stitches at the top of the buds using Appletons crewel wool No. 643. Fly stitch around the buds back to the stem with the same wool.

Embroider the wool rose leaves using Appletons tapestry wool No. 644.

10. *Section 10* Embroider the straight stitch flowers with three petals in Anchor tapestry wool No. 8832 and two petals in Anchor tapestry wool No. 8836.
Flower centres – 1 colonial knot, Gold Rush No. X2.
Leaves – 2 lazy daisy stitches, Appletons crewel wool No. 295.

11. *Section 11* Embroider the lazy daisy flowers first using Appletons tapestry wool No. 841. Embroider the buds next in the same wool and lazy daisy stitch. Embroider the centres of the flowers using DMC Perle 3 No. 3045 and three colonial knots.

Embroider the continuous fly stitch fern using Appletons crewel wool No. 643. Fly stitch with the same wool around the buds.

12. *Section 12* Embroider the seven groups of colonial knots first. These form the centres of the lazy daisy flowers:
Flower 1 – Appletons tapestry wool No. 694.
Flower 2 – Appletons tapestry wool No. 692.
Flower 3 – Appletons tapestry wool No. 841.
Flower 4 – Appletons tapestry wool No. 692.
Flower 5 – Appletons tapestry wool No. 841.
Flower 6 – Appletons tapestry wool No. 692.
Flower 7 – Appletons tapestry wool No. 841.

Embroider the lazy daisy petals all around the knots using Appletons crewel wool No. 643.

Embroider one colonial knot for each of the buds using Appletons crewel wool No. 693, and fly stitch around the buds with Appletons crewel wool No. 295.

13. *Section 13* Embroider the lazy daisy flowers using Anchor tapestry wool No. 8832. Embroider the centre of the flowers next with four colonial knots using Gold Rush No. X2.

Embroider the lazy daisy buds using the same wool as the flowers. Embroider the fly stitch around the buds using Appletons crewel wool No. 295.

Embroider the continuous fly stitch fern using Appletons crewel wool No. 295.

14. *Section 14* Embroider the buttonhole flowers using Appletons crewel wool No. 693. Embroider the buds and knots with DMC stranded cotton No. 729, using 6 strands. Embroider the leaves and stem using Appletons crewel wool No. 643.

To make up covered basket:

To wash the basket cover, just remove the template plastic and wash the cover by hand. Drip dry, and iron the embroidered lid on a towel when dry (see page 3).

Wash the cotton basket lining fabric, and then cut one base using the pattern on page 73. Seam allowances on the pattern are 12 mm ($^1$/2"). 

Cut two lining lids using the pattern on page 74.

1. Cut two pieces of cotton fabric, 35.5 cm x 115 cm (14" x 45"), for the 'frill'.

2. Take the two pieces of frill and machine together 18 cm (7") of the seam at each end using 2.5 cm, or 1", seams. Do not sew the bottom section (diag. 1).

3. Turn the unstitched section back on the seam allowance and machine stitch (diag. 2).

4. Divide the base section into quarters and leave a pin at each quarter marking.

5. Take the joined piece of frill and stitch two rows of gathering stitches around the top section (diag. 3).

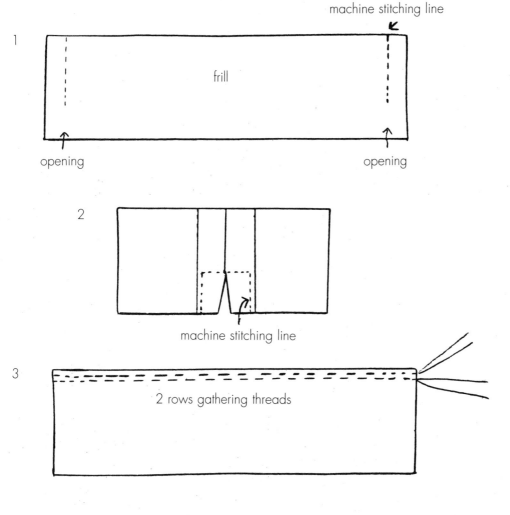

machine stitching line

1

frill

opening                    opening

2

machine stitching line

3

2 rows gathering threads

6. Divide the frill section into quarters. Leave a pin in at the quarter markings. Gather the frill section up to fit the base.

   The right side of the base and the right side of the frill should be facing one another. Place one seam of the frill on the quarter section of the base side marked A. Place the other seam on the other side of the base marked B. The other two quarter sections should now match up with the pins.

   Pin the frill completely around the base piece and machine in place using a 12 mm ($^1/_2$") seam. Overlock or oversew the edges together.

7. Overlock or oversew around the raw edge of the frill. Now flat sew the lace to the edge of the frill. Do not sew any lace around the openings (diag. 4).

8. Machine two buttonholes in the frill 6 cm (2.5") up from the lace edge and 12 mm ($^1/_2$") in from the fold. The buttonholes should measure 1.5 cm ($^5/_8$") in length. You should now have one buttonhole on each frill opposite each other (diag. 4).

9. On the wrong side of the frill and 5.5 cm (2 $^1/_4$") up from the lace edge, sew on the bias binding. Turn the edges of the bias binding under before you start. The bias binding starts 3 cm or (1 $^1/_4$") in from the folded edge and goes around to the same distance from the other end of the frill. Sew the bias binding on in two sections because of the openings (diag. 4).

10. Using a safety pin, thread a 65 cm (25 $^1/_2$") length of elastic through one of the bias binding casings. Secure the elastic at the ends when you have threaded it through with a few hand stitches. Repeat on the other half of the frill.

11. With a No. 9 crewel needle and strong sewing thread, sew the button on the frill 1.5 cm ($^5/_8$") in from the edge (diag. 5).

12. Take the two lining lids and fold the centre seam allowance back. (The seam allowance is 2.5 cm, or 1".) Sew the zipper into this opening.

13. Place the embroidered lid and the lining lid together, with wrong sides facing each other. Pin all around.

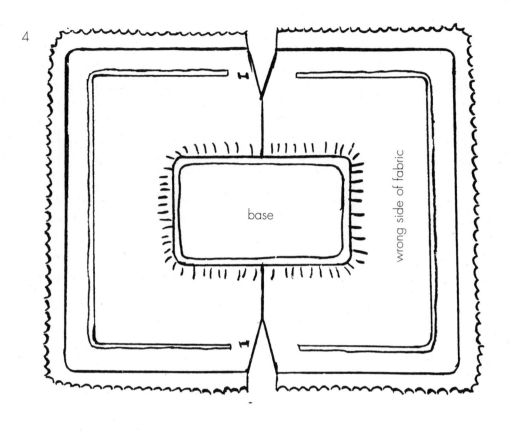

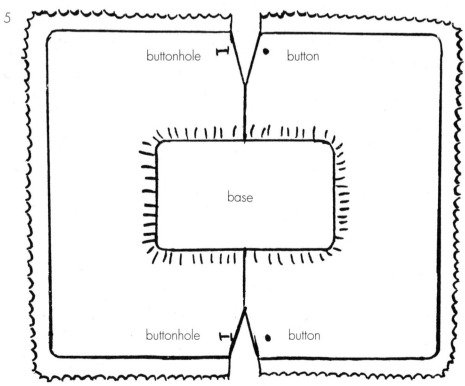

6

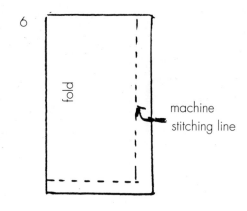

fold

machine
stitching line

7

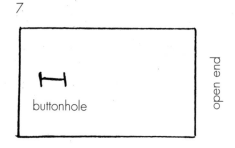

buttonhole

open end

8

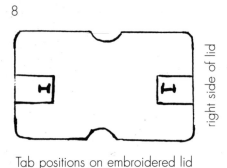

right side of lid

Tab positions on embroidered lid

14. Cut four pieces of cotton fabric, 7.5 cm x 7.5 cm (3"). Fold each piece in half with right sides facing, and machine down the long side and across the short side with 5 mm ($^1/_4$") seams (diag. 6).

　　Turn to the right side, through the unsewn opening. On two of these tabs, sew one buttonhole 1.5 cm ($^5/_8$") in length and 1.5 cm from the bottom sewn edge (diag. 7).

　　You should have two tabs with one buttonhole on each and two tabs with no buttonholes.

15. Find the centre of the embroidered lid. Now place one of the buttonholed tabs at the centre of each end of the embroidered lid (diag. 8).

16. Take the two tabs with no buttonholes in them and fold the top raw edges in. Sew these tabs to the right side of the frill in the centre, just above the bias binding stitch line. These tabs keep the lid in place when the basket is being carried. They also prevent things falling out of your basket. Sew the buttons onto the tabs 1.5 cm ($^5/_8$") from the bottom edge.

17. Overlock or oversew the embroidered lid and lining lid together. On the embroidered side of the lid, machine the lace on to cover the overlocking stitch.

18. Machine the ribbons to the lid on the side. These are used to tie the lid to the basket handle. I use double ribbons as they tie much better.

19. Cut the template plastic using the pattern on page 74. The dotted line on the pattern indicates the cutting line for the template plastic. Make sure you use the correct pattern piece as the size is very important. Unzip the zipper in the lining and slide one side of the template plastic in at a time. The lid is in two pieces so that it bends open more easily.

LAVENDER AND BULLION ROSES ON BERET AND SCARF

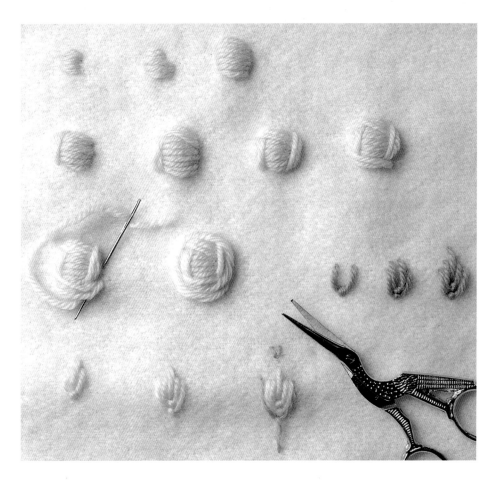

STEP-BY-STEP TO MAKING A WOOL ROSE, WOOL ROSE BUDS & WOOL ROSE LEAVES

BULLION ROSE BOUQUET ON LID OF JEWELLERY BOX, AND WOOL-EMBROIDERED JEWELLERY

BOUQUET OF CREAM CAMELLIAS ON KNEE RUG AND CUSHION

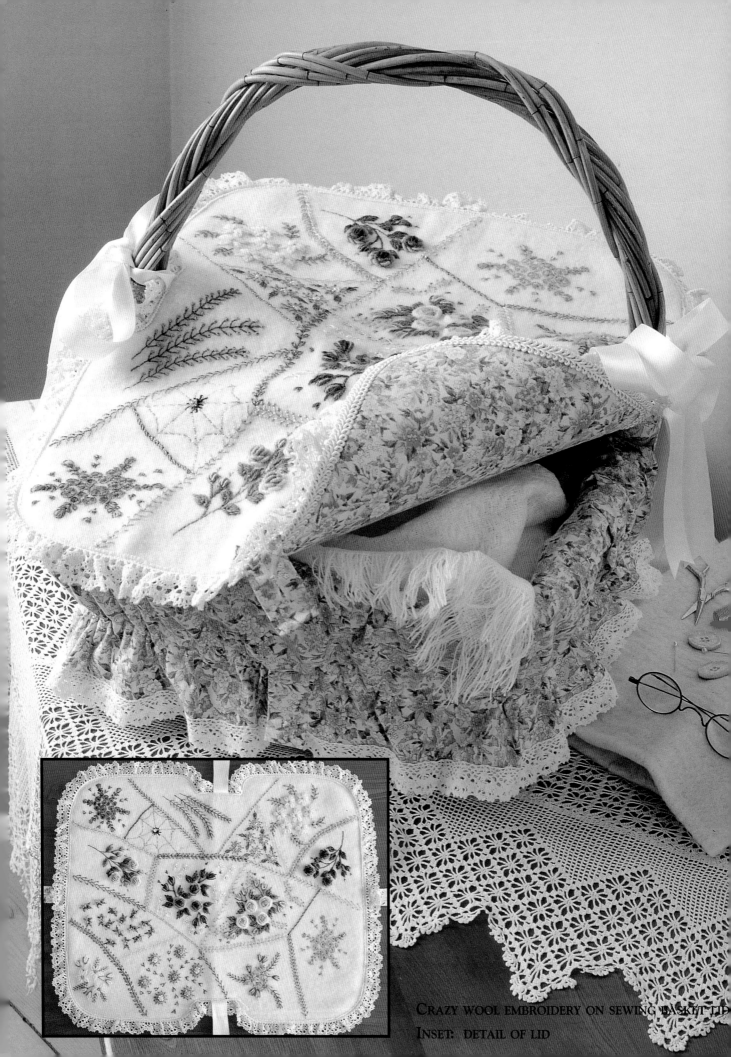

CRAZY WOOL EMBROIDERY ON SEWING BASKET LID

INSET: DETAIL OF LID

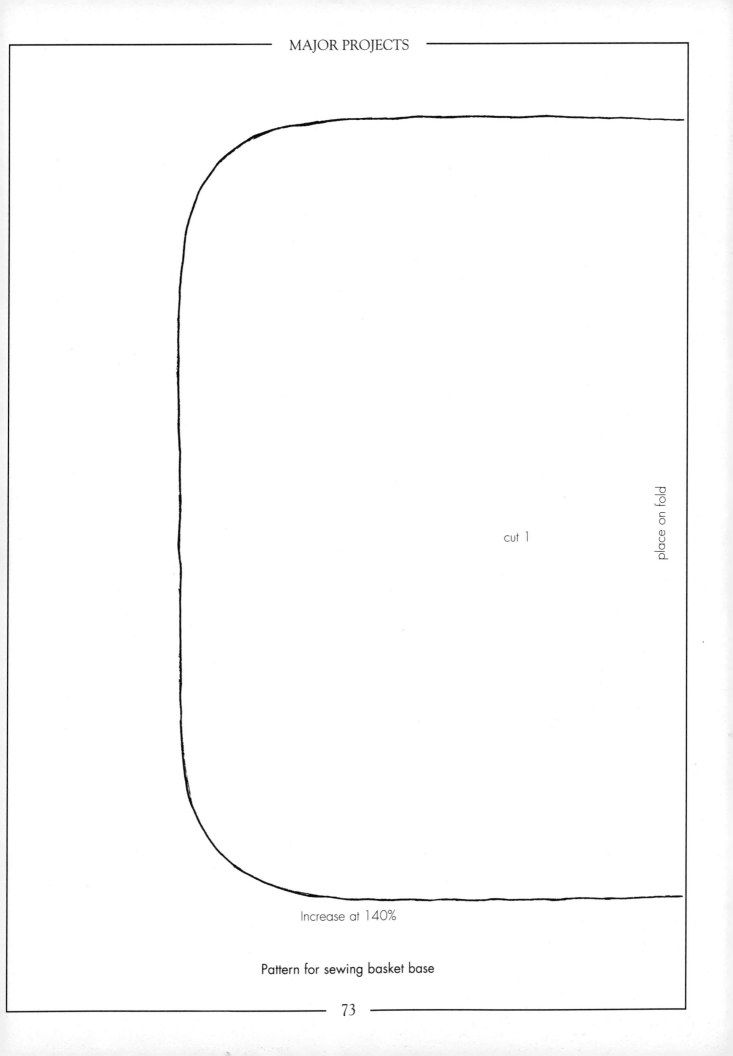

cut 1

place on fold

Increase at 140%

Pattern for sewing basket base

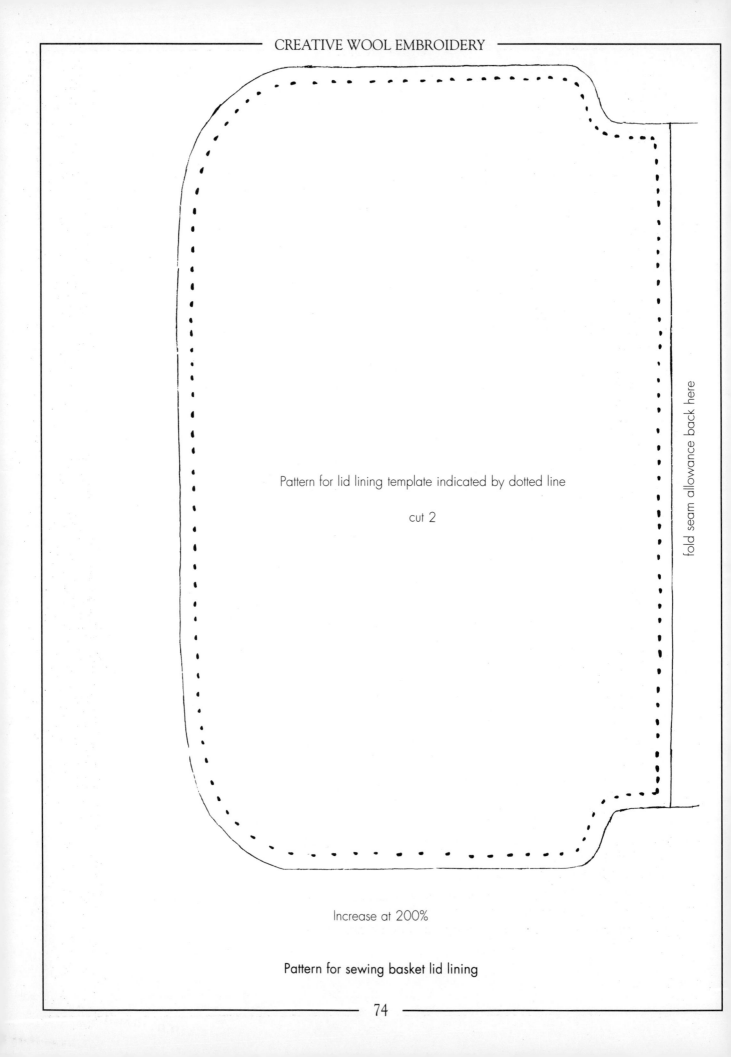

Pattern for lid lining template indicated by dotted line

cut 2

fold seam allowance back here

Increase at 200%

Pattern for sewing basket lid lining

*Greeting Card*

REQUIREMENTS
**Materials:**
Wool blanketing, 15 cm x 15 cm (6")
No. 18 chenille needles
No. 9 crewel needles
Small diamante bead for spider, 3 mm (1/8") in diameter

**Threads:**
Gold Rush No. X2
DMC Perle 5
– Nos 932, 501, 738 and 931
Anchor tapestry wool
– Nos 8838, 8836, 8832 and 9178
DMC stranded cotton
– Nos 310 and 729
Ribbon Floss No. 142 F-21
Appletons crewel wool
– Nos 295, 693 and 643
Appletons tapestry wool
– Nos 841 and 694

*Note:* If you have completed the embroidery for the sewing basket lid, you should not have to purchase any more threads.

To work section divider lines:

Using a water soluble pen, mark the outline of the opening in the card on the piece of wool fabric. Then mark the section dividing lines from the design chart on page 76 on the piece of wool blanketing.

1. Embroider Divider Line 1 first with Gold Rush No. X2 in chain stitch.
2. Embroider Divider Line 2 with DMC Perle 5 No. 932 in continuous fly stitch.
3. Embroider Divider Line 3 with DMC Perle 5 No. 501. Work a line of back stitches first and then come back and work a lazy daisy stitch either side of each back stitch.
4. Embroider Divider Line 4 next with DMC Perle 5 No. 738. Work in feather stitch and then come back and embroider a colonial knot on each spoke of the feather stitch.

To embroider flowers in each section:

1. *Section 1* Embroider the large bullion rose first, using 11 wraps for the bullion:
   1st row – Anchor tapestry wool No. 8838.
   2nd row – Anchor tapestry wool No. 8836.
   3rd row – Anchor tapestry wool No. 8832.
   Embroider the rose leaves using Anchor tapestry wool No. 9178.

2. *Section 2*  Embroider the spider's web in back stitch using Gold Rush No. X2. Sew the diamante on with a No. 9 crewel needle and cream sewing thread.

Using two strands of DMC stranded cotton No. 310 and straight stitches, embroider the spider's legs.

Each feeler is one pistil stitch and each eye is a colonial knot using two strands of DMC stranded cotton No. 310.

Embroider the pistil stitch flower in DMC Perle 5 No. 931. The centre of the flower consists of four colonial knots using Ribbon Floss No. 142 F-21. The leaves are fly stitched using Appletons crewel wool No. 295.

3. *Section 3*  Embroider the lazy daisy flower using Appletons tapestry wool No. 841. Tip the petals with a fly stitch using Appletons crewel wool No 693. The centre of the flower consists of one colonial knot in Appletons tapestry wool No. 694. Back stitch the leaf stems using Appletons crewel wool No. 643, and work the leaves in lazy daisy stitch using the same wool.

4. *Section 4*  Embroider the lazy daisy flowers using Anchor tapestry wool No. 8832. The centres of the flowers consist of four colonial knots in Gold Rush No. X2. The leaves are continuous fly stitch using Appletons crewel wool No. 295.

5. *Section 5*  Embroider the buttonhole flowers using Appletons crewel wool No. 693. Embroider the bud and knot in DMC stranded cotton No. 729, using 6 strands. Embroider the leaves and stems in Appletons crewel wool No. 643.

To make up the greeting card, refer to the instructions on page 49.

Actual size

Crazy Wool Embroidery – Greeting Card

## MINDI THE TEDDY BEAR

This bear stands 55 cm (22") in height. I do hope you love this bear as much as I do.

REQUIREMENTS

**Materials:**
Wool blanketing, 81 cm x 1 m (32" x 39")
No. 18 chenille needles
No. 9 crewel needles
4 cream buttons, 2.5 cm (1") in diameter with two holes in
  the top
Doll needles, 18 cm (7") long
Pair of 16 mm ($^5/_8$") glass eyes (*Note:* If the bear is for a child
  you should use buttons or safety eyes)
Toy filling, 2 kg (4 $^1/_2$ lb)
Fray Stopper
Cream double-sided satin ribbon, 1 m (39") x 2.5 cm (1") wide
Waxed dental floss
Small pearls
Gold heart

**Threads:**
Appletons tapestry wool
– Nos 472 (2 skeins), 841 (2 skeins), 871 (2 skeins),
  344 (2 skeins) and 992
Mary Hart-Davies pure silk (thick) No. 3
Kirra yarns Mohair No. 203
Ribbon Floss No. 144 F-10
Appletons crewel wool No. 842
DMC Medici No. 8308
DMC Perle 5 ecru cotton
DMC Perle 3
– Nos 726 and 842
DMC stranded cotton No. 310
Stonehouse Paterna wool No. 262

*Note:* In this project I have used No. 18 chenille needles for the embroidery and No. 9 crewel needles for sewing on the pearl beads and the gold heart.

The amount of wool used is only a guide. You might use more or less wool, depending on your tension.

**Stitches used:**
Satin stitch, stem stitch, fly stitch, straight stitch, lazy daisy stitch, continuous fly stitch and colonial knots.

Please read through the instructions carefully before starting. Seams of 5 mm ($^1/_4$") have been allowed on all pattern pieces. Make sure you mark out all the pieces before you start cutting.

Cut out the bear pattern pieces on pages 78 to 80. Note that you will have to enlarge these pieces.

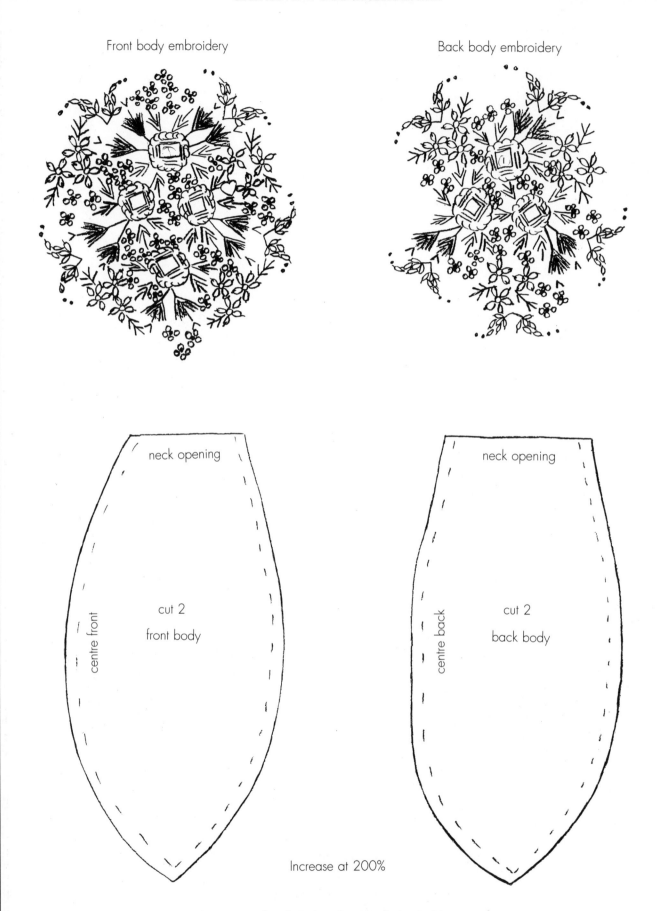

Front body embroidery

Back body embroidery

neck opening

neck opening

centre front

cut 2

front body

centre back

cut 2

back body

Increase at 200%

Patterns and embroidery for Mindi the Teddy Bear

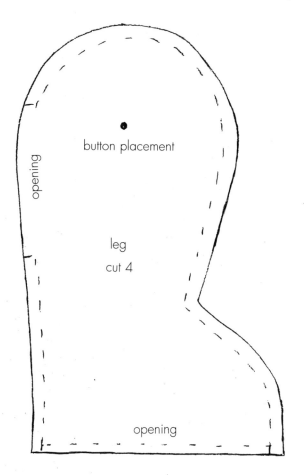

button placement

opening

leg

cut 4

opening

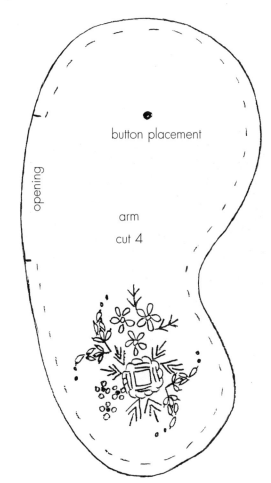

button placement

opening

arm

cut 4

Reverse design for other arm

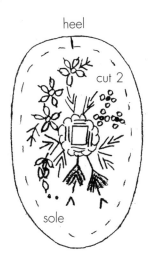

heel

cut 2

sole

ear

cut 4

opening

Reverse design for other ear

Increase at 200%

Pattern pieces have 5 mm (1/4") seam allowances

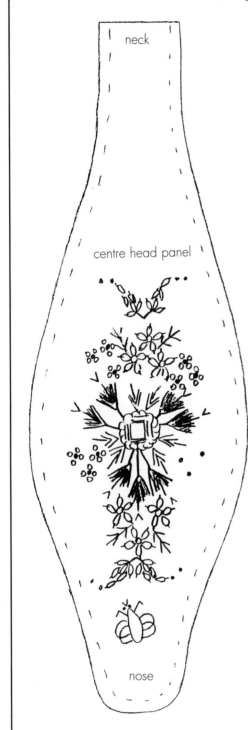

neck

centre head panel

nose

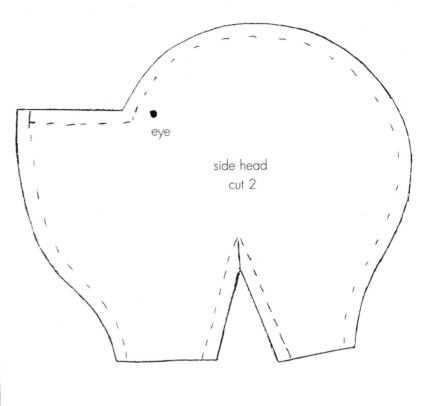

eye

side head
cut 2

Increase at 200%

1. Sew centre back body seam by hand or machine.

2. Sew centre front body seam by hand or machine.

3. Sew legs, leaving an opening between markings. Do not sew across bottom of leg.

4. Sew darts in the side head.

5. Sew nose seam in the side head.

To place and transfer designs:

Note that you will have to enlarge the embroidery designs. First of all, see page 3 for instructions on transferring designs. The embroidery patterns are positioned on the bear pieces as follows:

• *Ears and soles* Centre the embroidery. You will only embroider on two ear pieces. Make sure you have a right and a left ear. Also make sure you have the heel at the back of the sole.

• *Arms* Position the centre rose on the lower arm, making sure the embroidery does not go into the seams. You will only embroider on two arm pieces. Make sure you have a right and left arm.

- *Centre head panel* Place the centre rose 15 cm (6") from the bear's nose.

- *Back body* Place rose 1 on the seam line, 7.5 cm (3") down from the neck edge.

- *Front body* Place rose 1 on the seam line, 7.5 cm (3") down from the top neck edge.

To embroider *all* the pieces:

1. Embroider the wool roses first:
   1st row – Appletons tapestry wool No. 472.
   2nd row – Appletons tapestry wool No. 841.
   3rd row – Appletons tapestry wool No. 871.

2. Embroider the rose leaves using Appletons tapestry wool No. 344.

3. Embroider the rose buds:
   1st row – Appletons tapestry wool No. 472.
   2nd row – Appletons tapestry wool No. 871.
   3rd row – Appletons tapestry wool No. 344.

4. Embroider the blue lazy daisy flowers:
   Petals – Mary Hart-Davies pure silk (thick) No. 3.
   Leaves – continuous fly stitch, Kirra yarns Mohair No. 203.
   Centres – one pearl bead sewn on with a No. 9 crewel needle and cream sewing thread. Each pearl should be sewn on separately.

5. Embroider the forget-me-nots in Appletons tapestry wool No. 992 with four colonial knots. The centres consist of one colonial knot embroidered in Ribbon Floss No. 144 F-10.

6. Embroider the lavender using Appletons crewel wool No. 842. Stems are one fly stitch using DMC Medici No. 8308.

7. Embroider the bumble bee on the centre head panel (check directions in flower guide).

Embroider the pieces in the following order:
- Ears
- Soles
- Arms
- Centre head panel
- Back
- Front

Do not forget to sew the gold heart on the left front side with double sewing thread. All bears have hearts.

To make up Mindi:

*Note:* Pin all pieces before sewing.

1. Sew arms together by hand or machine, making sure you leave an opening where it is marked on the pattern. There will be one plain arm and one embroidered arm.

2. Sew around the ears leaving an opening where it is marked on the pattern. There will be one plain ear and one embroidered ear.

3. Sew the soles into the legs. Make sure the sole heel is on the back seam of the leg. I usually sew the soles in by hand using a small back stitch.

4. Sew the front side seams to the back side seams, leaving the neck edge open.

5. Sew the centre head panel into the head, starting at the nose. I usually tack the nose by hand first, and then machine in the centre head panel, one half at a time.

6. Fray Stopper all openings on both edges and leave to dry.

7. Turn legs, arms, body, ears and head to the right sides through the openings.

8. The bear's ears do not have any stuffing in them. Turn in the raw edges of the ears and oversew them.

9. Start stuffing the legs, arms, body and head. The secret of a good bear lies in the way it is stuffed. The firmer the stuffing, the better the bear will look. When you have stuffed all sections, ladder stitch openings together using DMC Perle 5 ecru cotton.

10. With DMC Perle 5 ecru, sew a running stitch around the top of the body opening, 5 mm (1/4") down from the raw edge, and draw in firmly. End the threads off securely.

11. Now sew a running stitch around the bottom of the head opening, 5 mm (1/4") up from the raw edge, and draw in firmly. End the threads off securely.

12. Match the side head and the side body and pin. Match the centre front head and the centre front body and pin. Match centre back head and centre back body and pin.

13. With DMC Perle 5 ecru, ladder stitch the head to the body.

14. Sew on the bear's legs and arms using double-waxed dental floss. It is difficult to pinpoint on a pattern just where to sew on the legs and arms. Place the legs and arms in position and when you are happy with the position, mark with a water soluble pen.

The legs and arms are sewn on with buttons and a doll needle. The buttons are on the outside of the legs and arms. Thread a doll needle with 1 m (39") of double dental floss. Tie a knot in the thread and anchor the thread on the inside of the arm. Pass the needle through the arm to the outside of the arm (the needle should come out at the spot you have marked with the water soluble pen). Take the needle through the button and pass the needle back through the arm, through the body, through the other arm and then through the button on that side of the bear. Then return the needle back through everything again, except when you get to the second arm, do not go through the button. Instead, bring the needle out under the button. Wrap the thread around your hand and pull it firmly. When you are satisfied that the arms are very firmly attached to the body, wrap the thread around the button and then end it off.

Secure the legs using the same method as for the arms.

15. Sewing on the bear's ears is a very important step. The positioning of the ears will determine your bear's personality. When you are happy with the ears' positions, pin them on. Ladder stitch the ears to the head, starting at the front of the ear and finishing at the back.

16. Embroider the nose using DMC Perle 3 No. 842 and a doll needle (diags 1 and 2). Begin with a knot in the centre of the nose in single thread. You will have to build up the layers until the nose is quite thick.

When you are happy with the nose, push the needle back under your stitches and begin to form the bear's mouth. Make one quite large fly stitch below the nose (diag. 3). To end the mouth off, tie a knot in the thread, take the needle back into the head and pull the thread through to the right side. Snip off close to the fabric and you will find that the thread disappears back into the head.

17. Sew the eyes on. (If the bear is for a baby you should use buttons or safety eyes.) The markings for the eyes are on the side head pattern.

For each eye, make a hole with a stiletto to place the eye in. If you don't do this, you may break the wire on your glass eyes, so it is important. Thread a piece of dental floss through the loop of the glass eye. Thread both ends through a doll needle and pass the needle through the eye marking and out at the centre back of the head at the base of the neck. Leave ends hanging.

Repeat the same step for the other eye. Bring the thread out close to the other eye thread. Tie both ends from eyes together in a reef knot to secure the eyes. Thread the remaining thread back through the head and snip off.

18. Tie a satin ribbon bow around the bear's neck.

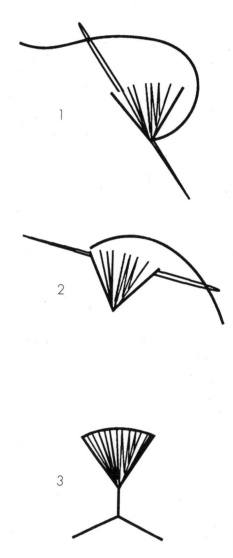

1

2

3

*Greeting Card*

To complete this embroidery, you will need a piece of wool blanketing, 11 cm x 16 cm (4 1/2" x 6 1/2"), plus the needles and threads listed for Mindi above. If you have made Mindi, you will have enough threads left over.

On the piece of blanketing, draw the outline of the opening in your card with a water soluble pen. Transfer the embroidery design chart below to the fabric.

To work the embroidery, follow the instructions for the embroidery of Mindi, steps 1 to 6.

To make up the greeting card, refer to the instructions given on page 49.

actual size

**Mindi the Teddy Bear – Greeting Card**

## STEM STITCH ROSES AND BUDS

*Elegant Doll Pin Cushion*

As well as being elegant, this doll pin cushion is very useful. I use mine all the time, and find that the gores on the top keep me organised. When I am working on a project, I keep all the needles of one size and type in one gore and all of those of another size and type in another gore.

It is a good idea to take your time with this project.

REQUIREMENTS

**Materials:**
Cream medium-weight woollen dress fabric:
– 1 circle, 33 cm (13") in diameter
– 1 piece, 20 cm (8") x 1.5 m (59") wide, for the skirt gores
– 2 circles, each 20 cm (8") in diameter
Cream double-sided satin ribbon, 2 pieces, 1 m (39") x 3 mm (1/8") wide
Toy filling or woollen scraps, 100 to 200 g (3 1/2 to 7 oz)
Plastic spray can lid
Cream braid, 70 cm (27 1/2")length
Craft glue
Porcelain half doll (this half doll was especially painted for this project and was purchased from Sarah Sey Dolls & Crafts, 39 Annangrove Road, Kenthurst, NSW 2156. Phone/Fax (02) 654 2181)
Dental floss
Size .6 mm crochet hook
No. 20 chenille needles
Mill Hill glass seed beads No. 00151

**Threads:**
DMC Perle 8 crochet cotton ecru (3 balls)
Kirra yarns Mohair
– Nos 325, 324, 216, 326 and 331
Patina No. PA257
DMC stranded cotton No. 524
Patina No. PA136

**Stitches used:**
Lazy daisy stitch, straight stitch, fly stitch, continuous fly stitch, stem stitch and colonial knots.

To crochet edges of underskirt:

Cut out the 33 cm (13") diameter circle from the woollen dress fabric. In the centre of the circle, cut out a 3.75 cm (1 1/2") diameter circle. Do not make this circle any smaller as it has to go over the doll. At this stage it a good idea to crochet the edges to prevent the fabric fraying when you are embroidering.

1. Crochet around the outer edge first. Sew a machine stitch around the edge about 3 mm ($^1$/$_8$") in from the raw edge. This machine stitch should be 2 mm in length. This line provides a good guide to keeping the double crochet evenly spaced. Work the crochet in DMC Perle 8 ecru and a .6 mm crochet hook:

   1st row – 1 double crochet into each hole.

   2nd row – 1 double crochet into the first stitch * 4 chain, miss 2 double crochet, 2 treble into the next double crochet, 4 chain, 2 treble into the same stitch, 4 chain, miss 2 double crochet, 1 double crochet into the next stitch repeat from *.

2. This time you will be crocheting around the smaller circle (the waist):

   1st row – 1 double crochet into each hole.

   2nd row – 1 double crochet into previous double crochet row.

   3rd row – 1 treble, 1 chain into each double crochet.

   4th row – 1 double crochet over each chain.

3. Take a metre (39") of the satin ribbon and weave it under and over the trebles around the waist of the underskirt. Leave ribbons hanging.

To embroider underskirt:

Transfer the underskirt design on page 87 onto the underskirt (see page 3).

1. Embroider the cream daisy flowers in Kirra yarns Mohair No. 331.

2. Embroider the continuous fly stitch fern using Patina No. PA136.

3. Embroider the small straight stitches over the ends of the lazy daisy petals using Patina No. PA136.

4. Embroider one colonial knot in the centre of each lazy daisy flower using Patina No. PA136.

To embroider gores of top skirt:

Cut 12 gores using the pattern on page 87. You do not have to allow seams. Only six gores are embroidered. Transfer the design on the pattern to the fabric.

1. Embroider stem stitch rose 1 first using Kirra yarns Mohair No. 325. Check flower and stitch guides for instructions on how to embroider the rose.

2. Embroider roses 2 and 3 using Kirra yarns Mohair No. 324.

3. Embroider the rose leaves in fly stitch using Kirra yarns Mohair No. 216.

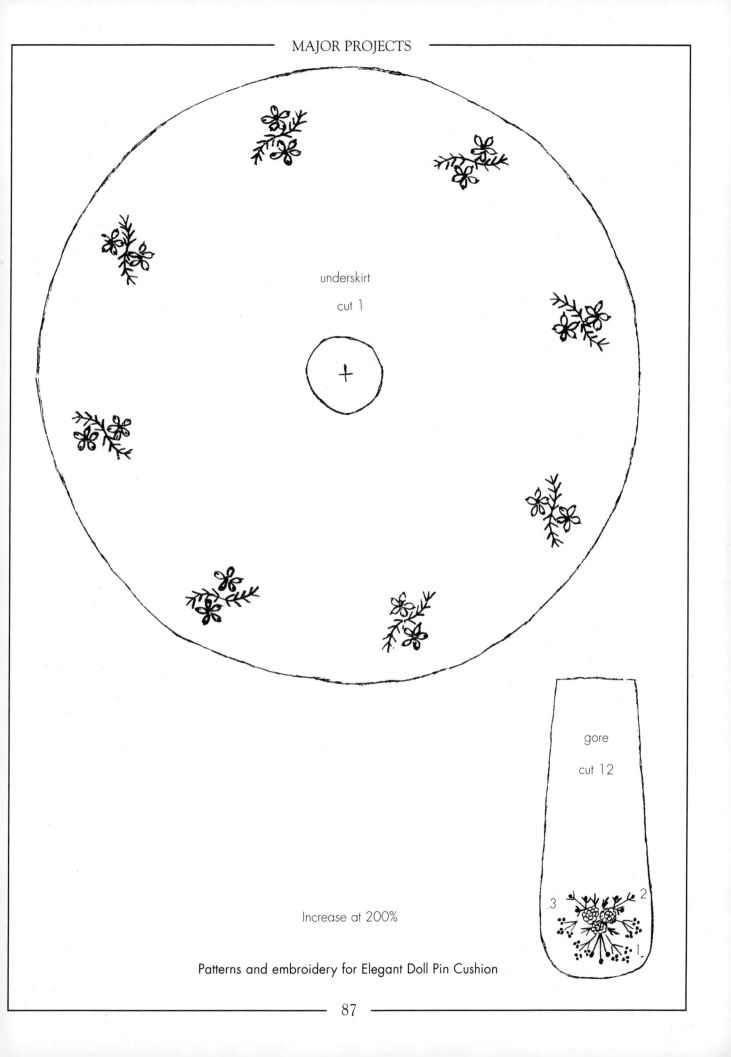

underskirt

cut 1

gore

cut 12

Increase at 200%

Patterns and embroidery for Elegant Doll Pin Cushion

4. Embroider the top buds next using Kirra yarns Mohair No. 326. The buds are worked in colonial knots.

5. Embroider the fly stitch around the buds using Kirra yarns Mohair No. 216. Take the fly stitch stem back to the rose to form the stem of the buds.

6. Embroider the bottom stems using Kirra yarns Mohair No. 216. The stems are straight stitches.

7. Embroider the bottom buds using Patina No. PA257. Each bud is one colonial knot.

8. Embroider the fine stems using one strand of DMC stranded cotton No. 524. Each stem is one fly stitch with a stem and one straight stitch in the centre.

9. Sew three Mill Hill glass seed beads No. 00151 on the tip of each fine stem. Each bead should be sewn on separately. Each set of fine stems has three sets of three beads, nine beads in total.

Repeat the same embroidery on the other five gores.

To crochet gores of top skirt:

Pin an embroidered gore on top of each of the plain gores. The right side of the embroidery should be facing up. Machine the two gores together about 3 mm ($^1/8$") in from the raw edge. If you do not have a sewing machine, you can double crochet straight away. The machine stitch is used as a guide so that you can make your double crochet evenly spaced.

1. Start the double crochet at the right-hand corner at the top of the gore:
   1st row – 1 double crochet all the way round and slip stitch into the first double crochet.
   2nd row – (working on the top of the gore now, making the eyelets to thread the ribbon through) 1 double crochet into each double crochet along the top.
   3rd row – 4 chain, (1 treble, 1 chain) to the end of the top edge, turn and 1 double crochet over each chain.
   4th row – 1 double crochet into the first stitch, * 4 chain, miss 2 double crochet, 2 treble into the next double crochet, 4 chain, 2 treble into the same stitch, 4 chain, miss 2 double crochet, 1 double crochet into the next stitch, repeat from *.

   Repeat the same crocheting around the other five gores.

2. Take the other metre (39") of satin ribbon and weave it under and over the trebles along the straight top edge of each gore. Leave ribbons hanging.

MINDI THE TEDDY BEAR WITH MATCHING GREETING CARD

ELEGANT DOLL PIN CUSHION AND EMBROIDERED NEEDLEBOOK.
INSET: FRONT OF NEEDLEBOOK

CHATELAINE EMBROIDERY WITH STEM STITCH ROSES AND BUDS

SUNFLOWER BALNKET AND CUSHION

To make pin cushion:

Cut out the two 20 cm (8") circles from the woollen fabric.

1. With a strong sewing thread doubled, work a small running stitch around one circle, about 12 mm ($^1$/2") in from the edge. Start with a knot in the thread and also take two or three overstitches to hold the thread firm. This thread has to withstand a great deal of strain, as it is used to gather in the edge. Do not end off the thread or cut off the needle.

2. Draw up the gathering thread until you have a very tight circle, secure with a couple of overstitches and then end off. Do not gather up the circle completely, as you have to stuff it with toy filling or woollen fabric scraps.

3. Start stuffing the toy filling or woollen fabric scraps into the circle through the hole in the back. You will end up with a large mushroom shape. Stuff the mushroom very firmly. Use the end of a wooden spoon to push the stuffing into the mushroom.

4. Place a few small rocks in the spray can lid. You can place some toy filling over the rocks to keep them in place.

5. Take the other woollen circle and, with a strong sewing thread doubled, work a small running stitch around this circle about 12 mm ($^1$/2") in from the edge. Once again, start with a knot in the thread and take two or three overstitches to hold the thread firm. This thread is also going to be used to gather in the edge. Do not end off this thread or cut off the needle.

6. Place the spray can lid inside the circle and gather the fabric in tightly. The fabric will come up over the top of the spray can lid. Secure the thread off with a couple of overstitches. This is the base.

7. With a chenille needle and matching strong thread, ladder stitch the mushroom to the base and end off securely.

8. Glue braid over the join of the mushroom and to the lower edge of the base.

To complete Elegant Doll Pin Cushion:

1. Centre the half doll on top of the pin cushion and, using dental floss and the holes in the bottom of the half doll, sew on the half doll very firmly.

2. Now lower the underskirt over the doll's head and tie it firmly around the lower part of the doll's waist at the back with the satin ribbon. Leave the long tails of the ribbon hanging.

3. Take the top skirt, which consists of the six gores, and tie it around the doll's waist on top of the underskirt. Make sure the ribbon ties are at the back of the doll. You can cut the ties to whatever length you would like them. I usually leave mine long.

## Embroidered Needle Book

This is a very useful project. You will always know where your needles are and what size they are. Once again, I would suggest you take your time on this project.

REQUIREMENTS

**Materials:**
Cream medium-weight woollen dress fabric, 80 cm (31 $^1/2$") x 150 cm (59") wide
Fine cotton fabric, 25 cm (10") length
Template plastic, 2 sheets
Pearl button with 10 mm ($^3/8$") diameter shank
No. 20 chenille needles
No. 10 crewel needles
Size .6 mm crochet hook
Mill Hill glass seed beads No. 00151

**Threads:**
Kirra yarns Mohair
– Nos 330, 324, 325, 216, 326 and 331
DMC stranded cotton No 524
Patina No. PA257
Patina No. PA136
DMC Perle 8 crochet cotton ecru (4 balls)

**Stitches used:**
Whipped chain stitch, stem stitch, fly stitch, colonial knots, straight stitch, lazy daisy stitch and continuous fly stitch.

To embroider cover:

Cut two pieces of cream woollen fabric using the cover pattern on page 92. You will only embroider one of these pieces. Transfer the front cover design on the pattern to one half of one of the pattern pieces (see page 3). In this project I would suggest you transfer small sections at a time.

1. Embroider the border first using Kirra yarns Mohair No. 330 and whipped chain.

2. Embroider your initial next using Kirra yarns Mohair No. 330 and whipped chain. You can draw your own initial or trace one from an initial book. Mine was drawn freehand. You can also embroider a couple of stem stitch roses in your initial. Position the roses wherever you like. Check the flower and stitch guides for the rose instructions. Use Kirra yarns Mohair No. 324 for one rose and Kirra yarns Mohair

No. 325 for the other. You can choose where and what colour when you embroider your own initial.

3. *Corner sections* Embroider stem stitch rose 1 first using Kirra yarns Mohair No. 325. Check flower and stitch guides for instructions on how to embroider the rose. Embroider roses 2 and 3 using Kirra yarns Mohair No. 324.

Embroider the rose leaves in fly stitch using Kirra yarns Mohair No. 216.

Embroider the buds using Kirra yarns Mohair No. 326. The buds are worked in colonial knots.

Embroider the fly stitch around the buds using Kirra yarns Mohair No. 216. Take the fly stitch stem back to the rose to form the stem of the buds.

Embroider the fine stems next using one strand of DMC stranded cotton No. 524. These stems are one fly stitch with a stem and one straight stitch in the centre.

Sew three Mill Hill glass seed beads No. 00151 on the tip of each fine stem. Sew on each bead separately. Each set of fine stems has three sets of three beads, nine beads in total.

Repeat on the other three corners.

4. Write 'Needles' with a water soluble pen at the bottom of the design. Embroider this word in whipped chain stitch using two strands of DMC stranded cotton No. 524.

5. *Centre top rose section* Embroider stem stitch rose 1 first using Kirra yarns Mohair No. 324. Embroider rose 2 using Kirra yarns Mohair No. 325. Embroider roses 3 and 4 using Kirra yarns Mohair No. 324.

Embroider the rose leaves in fly stitch using Kirra yarns Mohair No. 216.

Embroider the three stems for the top buds using Kirra yarns Mohair No. 216 and straight stitches. Now embroider the top three buds using Patina No. PA257 (each bud is one colonial knot).

Embroider the bottom buds next using Kirra yarns Mohair No. 326. The buds are worked in colonial knots.

Embroider the fly stitch around the buds and the fine stems, and sew on the glass beads (see instructions above, step 3).

6. *Section under your initial* Embroider rose 1 first using Kirra yarns Mohair No. 325. Embroider roses 2 and 3 next using Kirra yarns Mohair No. 324.

Embroider the rose leaves in fly stitch using Kirra yarns Mohair No. 216.

Embroider the top buds using Kirra yarns Mohair No. 326. The buds are worked in colonial knots.

Embroider the fly stitch around the buds using Kirra yarns Mohair No. 216. Take the fly stitch stem back to the rose to form the stem of the buds.

place on fold

cut 2

Increase at 140%

Pattern and embroidery for Embroidered Needle Book cover

Embroider the three stems for the bottom buds using Kirra yarns Mohair No. 216. The stems are straight stitches.

Embroider one colonial knot (one bud) on each stem using Patina No. PA257.

Embroider the fine stems next and sew on the glass beads (see instructions above, step 3).

7. *Side rose sections* Embroider rose 1 first using Kirra yarns Mohair No. 325. Embroider roses 2 and 3 next using Kirra yarns Mohair No. 324.

Embroider the fly stitch rose leaves using Kirra yarns Mohair No. 216.

Embroider the buds next using Kirra yarns Mohair No. 326. The buds are worked in colonial knots.

Embroider the fly stitch around the buds and the fine stems, and sew on the glass beads (see instructions above, step 3).

Repeat in the opposite section.

8. *Lazy daisy sections* Embroider the cream lazy daisy flowers next using Kirra yarns Mohair No. 331. Embroider the buds in the same wool and one lazy daisy petal.

Embroider the fern using Patina No. PA136. The fern is embroidered in continuous fly stitch. Embroider one fly stitch around the bud.

Embroider small straight stitches over the ends of the lazy daisy petals and the buds with Patina No. PA136.

Embroider a colonial knot in the centre of each lazy daisy using Patina No. PA136.

9. Transfer the lazy daisies design to the other half of your embroidered piece (this is the back cover of the needle book). Now follow step 8 above.

*actual size*
**Embroidery for back cover**

To crochet and attach pockets:

These pockets are for the pages of the needle book. Cut two pieces of wool fabric using the pages pattern on page 95. Cut 12 pieces of woollen fabric, 16 cm x 6 cm (6 $^1/4$" x 2 $^1/4$"), for the pockets. Cut 12 pieces of fine cotton fabric the same size.

1. Pin one piece of woollen pocket fabric and one piece of cotton fabric together. Machine a line of stitching all around the fabric, 3 mm ($^1/8$") in from the edge.

2. Work the crocheting all around the edge of the pocket in DMC Perle 8 ecru and a .6 mm crochet hook:
1st row – 1 double crochet into each hole.
2nd row – 1 double crochet into the first stitch, * 4 chain, miss 2 double crochet, 2 treble into the next double crochet, 4 chain, 2 treble into the same stitch, 4 chain, miss 2 double crochet, 1 double crochet into the next stitch, repeat from *.

Make 11 more of these pockets in the same manner as above.

3. To attach crocheted pockets onto pages, take one page piece of woollen fabric and lay it flat down on the table. Lay the pockets onto the page in the positions shown on the page pattern piece (page 95).

Machine around the outside edge but not along the top edge. Now machine in the dividing sections (as shown on the pattern).

Make sure you sew crocheted pockets onto the inside cover of your needle book. The pockets will be the same size, but the inside cover will be a different size from that of the pages See page 95 for the positions of the pockets on the inside cover.

To prepare and crochet pages:

Cut two pieces of template plastic using the template page pattern on page 95. The plastic is slightly smaller so that you do not sew it by the machine. The plastic is cut in two so that the page will bend easily.

1. Take two page pieces of woollen fabric with the pockets sewn on them and place the two wrong sides together. Sandwich the template plastic in between the two pages. The right side of your pages should be on the outside. Pin together and then hand tack around where you have pinned. This will stop the plastic moving when you are machining it.

2. You are now ready to crochet around the page. For each of the pages, follow step 2 on page 93 for crocheted edge.

To prepare and crochet cover:

Cut two pieces of template plastic using the template cover pattern on page 95. The plastic is slightly smaller than the cover to avoid sewing it by the machine.

1. Take the embroidered cover and the prepared inside cover and place the two wrong sides together. The right side of the embroidered cover and the right side of the inside cover should be facing out. Sandwich the template plastic between the outside cover and the inside cover and pin all around. Make sure the inside cover is not upside down (the pocket openings should be at the top). Hand tack around where you have pinned the fabrics together. This will stop the plastic moving when you are machining it. Machine a line of stitching 3 mm ($1/8$") in from the edge.

2. You are now ready to crochet around the cover. Follow step 2 on page 93 for crocheted edge.

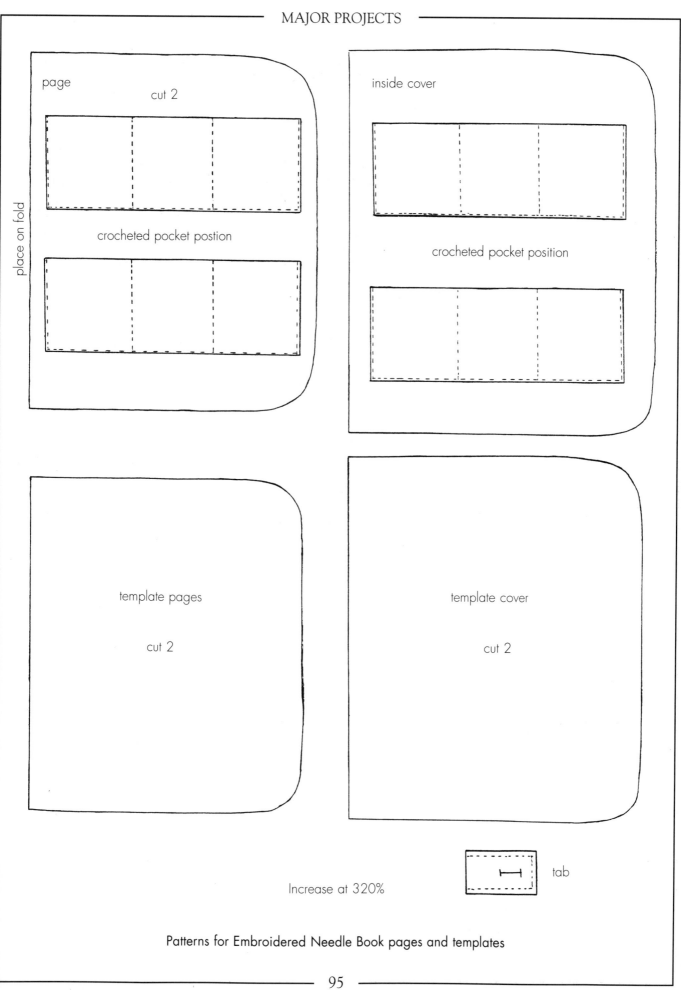

page
cut 2

place on fold

crocheted pocket postion

inside cover

crocheted pocket position

template pages

cut 2

template cover

cut 2

Increase at 320%

tab

Patterns for Embroidered Needle Book pages and templates

To crochet and attach tab:

First of all, make up the tab. Cut a piece of woollen fabric 9 cm x 2.5 cm (3 1/2" x 1"). Fold the fabric in half so that the tab ends up 4.5 cm x 2.5 cm (1 3/4" x 1").

1. Machine one buttonhole in the tab as shown in the diagram on page 95. The size of the buttonhole will depend on the size of the buttons. My buttonhole measures 12 mm (1/2"). Make sure your button will go through the buttonhole. Machine a line of stitching around the tab 3 mm (1/8") in from the edge.

2. Now crochet around this tab. Follow step 2 on page 93 for crocheted edge. Only crochet three sides (do not crochet across the fold).

3. Find the centre of the embroidered cover on the opening edge. You will have to measure it with a tape measure. Hand sew the tab to the inside cover, 5 mm (1/4") in from the edge. Sew on the button to the back cover, 5 mm in from the edge in the centre.

To complete Needle Book:

1. Lay the needle book cover flat on the table with the embroidered side facing the table. Take the completed page and lay the page on top of the inside cover of the needle book. Make sure the page is not upside down, by checking that the pockets have their openings at the top.

2. Pin through the centre of both pieces, between the template plastic. Hand tack them together and then machine them together.

3. I have added a tassel (made by Su-Lee Oei) to my needle book as a decorative extra.

*Embroidered Chatelaine* _____

There is a lot of work involved in making this project, but it is very beautiful when it is finished – a real heirloom. I have always wanted a chatelaine that can be worn around the waist rather than the neck. In the old days the housekeeper always wore the chatelaine around her waist. Chatelaines then were made from either Hallmarked silver or brass. Today these metal chatelaines are very rare. I saw a beautiful one made in Hallmarked silver about ten years ago, and I guess that chatelaine was on my mind when I was designing this one. This chatelaine has the same advantages as the old metal ones, in that you can wear it around your waist comfortably and use the pieces as you need them, or detach all the pieces and place them on the table when you are working with them.

REQUIREMENTS

**Materials:**

Cream medium-weight woollen dress fabric, 65 cm (25 $^1/2$") x 150 cm (59") wide

Toy filling or scraps of wool blanketing

9 pearl buttons with a shank 10 mm ($^3/8$") in diameter

Template plastic, 1 sheet

Very fine cord, 40 cm (15 $^3/4$") length, or double-sided cream satin ribbon, 40 cm x 3 mm ($^1/8$") wide

Medium-weight interfacing, 15 cm (6") length

Size .6 mm crochet hook

No. 20 chenille needles

No. 10 crewel needles

Mill Hill glass seed beads No. 00151 (2 pkts)

**Threads:**

DMC Perle 8 crochet cotton ecru (5 balls)

Kirra yarns Mohair
– 2 skeins each of Nos 324, 325, 216, 326, 331 and 330

Patina No. PA257 (2 cards)

Patina No. PA136 (2 cards)

DMC stranded cotton No. 524 (2 skeins)

**Stitches used:**

Stem stitch, fly stitch, colonial knots, straight stitch, lazy daisy stitch, continuous fly stitch and whipped chain.

To make and crochet tabs:

The tabs are where you sew your button or where the buttonhole is sewn. You should cut them all out and then make up a couple at a time. Cut 13 tabs out of your woollen fabric, each 9 cm x 2.5 cm (3 $^1/2$" x 1"). Fold the fabric in half so that the tabs end up 4.5 cm x 2.5 cm (1 $^3/4$" x 1").

1. Take seven of the tabs and machine one buttonhole in each tab as shown on the needle book pattern on page 108. The size of the buttonhole will depend on the size of your buttons. My buttonhole measures 12 mm ($^1/2$"). Make sure the button will go through the buttonhole. Machine a line of stitching around each tab 3 mm ($^1/8$") in from the edge.

2. Take the other six tabs and machine a line of stitching around each tab 3 mm ($^1/8$") in from the edge. These tabs do not have any buttonholes in them.

3. Now it is time to crochet around each tab. Follow step 2 in the section called 'To crochet and attach pockets' in the Needle Book, page 93, for crocheted edge. However, before you crochet the edge, crochet two rows of double crochet. Only crochet around three sides of the tab, not along the folded edge. When you have completed the tabs, put them to one side for later.

**Pin Cushion**

To embroider front:

Cut one piece of woollen fabric, 10 cm x 10 cm (4"). Transfer the design on page 99 to this fabric, centring the design on the fabric (see page 3).

1. Embroider roses 1, 2, 3 and 4 first using Kirra yarns Mohair No. 324.

2. Embroider roses 5 and 6 using Kirra yarns Mohair No. 325.

3. Embroider the fly stitch rose leaves using Kirra yarns Mohair No. 216.

4. Embroider the side buds on the roses using Kirra yarns Mohair No. 326. The buds are worked in colonial knots.

5. Embroider the fly stitch around the buds using Kirra yarns Mohair No. 216. Take the fly stitch stem back to the rose to form the stem of the bud.

6. Embroider the straight stitch stems at the top and bottom of the roses using Kirra yarns Mohair No. 216.

7. Embroider the buds on the straight stitch stems (one colonial knot on each stem) using Patina No. PA257.

8. Embroider the cream lazy daisy flowers using Kirra yarns Mohair No. 331. Embroider the buds in the same wool. Each bud is one lazy daisy petal.

9. Embroider the continuous fly stitch fern using Patina No. PA136. Embroider one fly stitch around the bud.

10. Embroider small straight stitches over the ends of the lazy daisy petals and the buds with Patina No PA136.

11. Embroider one colonial knot in the centre of each lazy daisy flower using Patina No. PA136.

12. Embroider the fine stems using one strand of DMC stranded cotton No. 524. These stems consist of one fly stitch with a stem and one straight stitch in the centre.

13. Sew three Mill Hill glass seed beads No. 00151 on the tip of each fine stem. Sew each bead on separately. Each set of fine stems has three sets of three beads, nine beads in total.

To embroider back:

Cut two pieces of woollen fabric, each 7.5 cm x 10 cm (3" x 4"), to form back of pin cushion using the pattern on page 99. Fold back a 2.5 cm (1") seam. The fabric now should measure 5 cm x 10 cm (2" x 4").

Find the centre of the fabric and transfer the design on page 99.

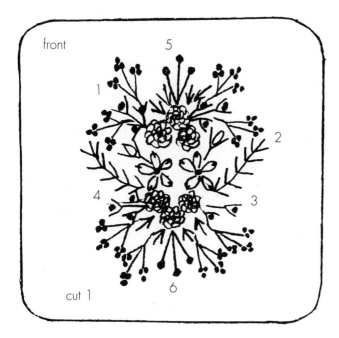

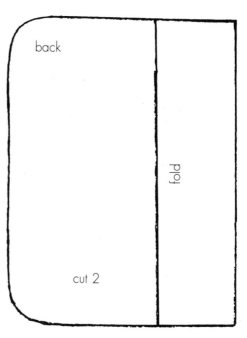

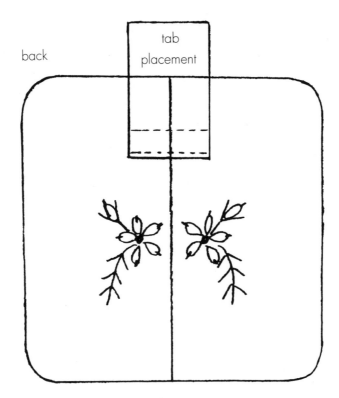

Increase at 130%

Patterns and embroidery for pin cushion

1. Embroider the lazy daisy flower on the right side first, taking your stitches through the seam allowance. Work the petals in lazy daisy stitch using Kirra yarns Mohair No. 331. Embroider the buds in the same wool. Each bud is one lazy daisy petal.

2. Embroider the continuous fly stitch fern using Patina No. PA136. Embroider one fly stitch around the bud.

3. Embroider small straight stitches over the ends of the lazy daisy petals and the buds with Patina No. PA136.

4. Embroider one colonial knot in the centre of each lazy daisy flower using Patina No. PA136.

To make up and crochet pin cushion:

1. Take the two back pieces and place the folded edges towards each other. The fabric should be flat. Now position one of the tabs without a buttonhole in it as shown in the diagram on page 99.

   Pin the tab in place and machine across the folded edge of the tab. The crocheted edge should be on the top edge. You can sew a second row of stitching 5 mm ($1/4$") above the previous row of stitching.

2. Take the front embroidered fabric and the back embroidered fabric and place the wrong sides together. Pin all around and sew a machine stitch 3 mm ($1/8$") in from the edge. Leave the back folded seam open at this stage.

3. You are now ready to crochet around the edge. Follow step 2 in section called 'To crochet and attach pockets' in the Needle Book, page 93, for crocheted edge.

4. Push the toy filling or wool scraps in through the opening in the back of the pin cushion. (I prefer to use scraps of pure wool to fill my pin cushion.) The amount of stuffing is your choice.

5. When your pin cushion is stuffed to your satisfaction, ladder stitch the opening closed.

6. Sew a button on the front of the tab, 12 mm ($1/2$") down from the crocheted edge.

*Note:* When cutting out each shaped Chatelaine piece, do not cut out the exact shape as it will be too small to machine around. You should draw your shape onto your fabric and then cut around it roughly, as in the diagram.

   You do not have to cut your back pieces out exactly either. It will make it a lot easier when you sandwich the template plastic in between the two pieces of woollen fabric.

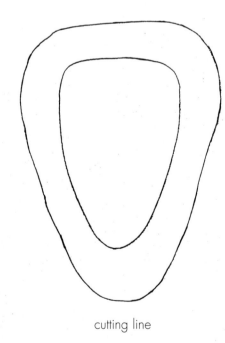

cutting line

**Scissor Case**

To embroider front section:

Cut two pieces of woollen fabric out roughly for front of scissor case, using the pattern on page 103. You will be embroidering on only one of these pieces. Transfer the design on the pattern to the fabric.

1.  Embroider roses 1, 2, 3, 4 and 5 first using Kirra yarns Mohair No. 324.

2.  Embroider roses 6 and 7 next using Kirra yarns Mohair No. 325.

3.  Embroider the fly stitch rose leaves using Kirra yarns Mohair No. 216.

4.  Embroider the side buds top and bottom using Kirra yarns Mohair No. 326. The buds are worked in colonial knots.

5.  Embroider the fly stitch around the side buds using Kirra yarns Mohair No. 216. Take the fly stitch stem back to the rose to form the stem of the bud.

6.  Embroider the straight stitch stems at the top and bottom of the roses using Kirra yarns Mohair No. 216.

7.  Embroider the buds on the straight stitch stems (one colonial knot on each stem) using Patina No. PA257.

8.  Embroider the cream lazy daisy flowers using Kirra yarns Mohair No. 331. Embroider the buds in the same wool. Each bud is one lazy daisy petal.

9.  Embroider the continuous fly stitch fern using Patina No. PA136. Embroider one fly stitch around the bud.

10. Embroider small straight stitches over the ends of the lazy daisy petals and the buds with Patina No PA136.

11. Embroider one colonial knot in the centre of each lazy daisy flower using Patina No. PA136.

12. Embroider the fine stems and sew on the beads, following steps 12 and 13 of the instructions for embroidering the front of the pin cushion, page 98.

To embroider back section:

Cut two pieces of woollen fabric for the back scissor case using the pattern on page 103. Leave the rough edge the same as for the front scissor case. Transfer the design on the back pattern to the fabric. Make sure you centre the design.

1. Embroider the cream lazy daisy flowers using Kirra yarns Mohair No. 331. Embroider the buds in the same wool. Each bud is one lazy daisy petal.

2. Embroider the continuous fly stitch fern using Patina No. PA136. Embroider one fly stitch around the bud.

3. Embroider small straight stitches over the ends of the lazy daisy petals and the buds with Patina No. PA136.

4. Embroider one colonial knot in the centre of each lazy daisy flower using Patina No. PA136.

To assemble and crochet front scissor case:

Cut one piece of template plastic using the front template pattern on page 103.

1. Now sandwich the template plastic in between the embroidered front of the scissor case and the piece of plain fabric. Pin around the markings of the front scissor case. Hand tack these two pieces of fabric together so that the template plastic will not slip when you are machining around it. Machine around the markings.

2. Cut away the excess fabric leaving a 2 mm ($1/8$") seam allowance from the machine stitching.

3. Use DMC Perle 8 crochet cotton ecru and a .6 mm crochet hook to crochet all the way around the front scissor case:
   1st row – 1 double crochet all the way around.
   2nd row – Crochet another double crochet all the way around the edge.
   3rd row – 1 double crochet into the first stitch, * 4 chain, miss 2 double crochet, 2 treble into the next double crochet, 4 chain, 2 treble into the same stitch, 4 chain, miss 2 double crochet, 1 double crochet into the next stitch, repeat from *.

To assemble and crochet back scissor case:

Cut one piece of template plastic using the back template pattern on page 103.

1. Take the back embroidered scissor case and one of the tabs without a buttonhole in it and position the tab as shown on the back pattern on page 103. Pin the tab in place and sew on by machine across the folded edge of the tab. The crocheted edge should be on the top. You can sew a second row of stitching 5 mm ($1/4$") above the previous row of stitching.

2. Now take the back embroidered scissor case and the piece of plain woollen fabric. Sandwich the template plastic in between the embroidered fabric and the plain fabric. Pin around the markings of the back scissor case. Hand tack these two pieces of fabric together so that the template plastic will not slip when you are machining around it. Machine around the markings.

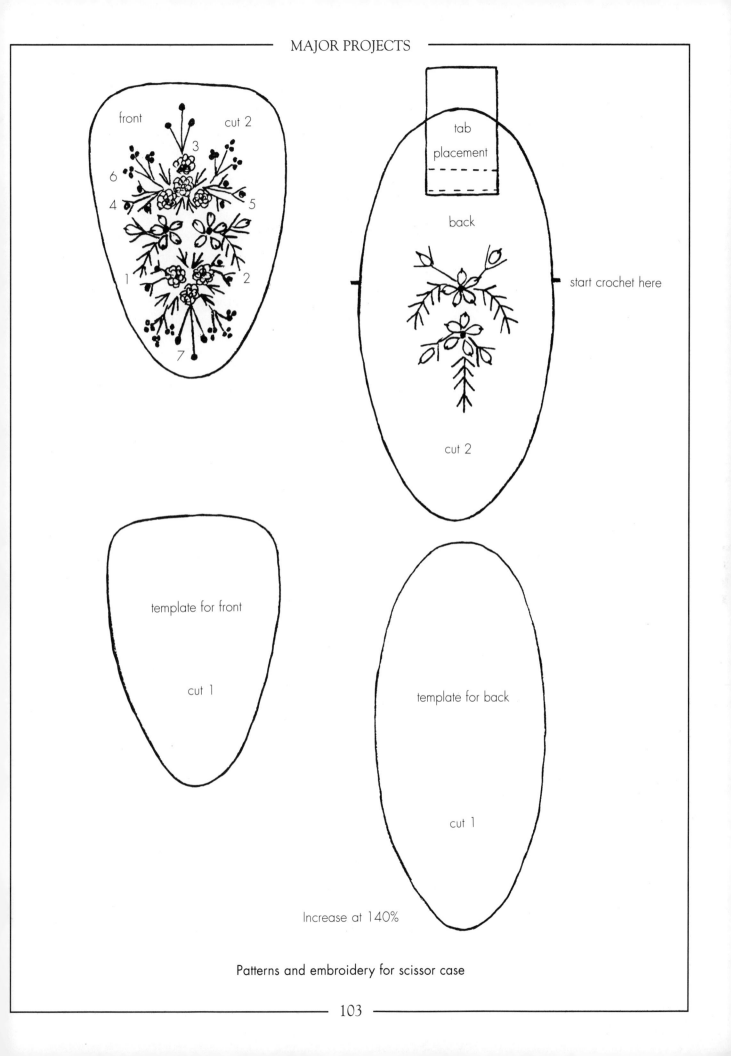

front

cut 2

3

6

4

5

1

2

7

tab

placement

back

start crochet here

cut 2

template for front

cut 1

template for back

cut 1

Increase at 140%

Patterns and embroidery for scissor case

3. Cut away the excess fabric leaving a 3 mm ($^{1}/8"$) seam allowance from the machine stitching.

4. Use DMC Perle 8 crochet cotton ecru and a .6 mm crochet hook to crochet the edge. It is very important that you start the first row of double crochet where I have marked it. It is not necessary to crochet the fancy edge all around the back scissor case, only around the top.
   1st row – 1 double crochet all the way around the edge.
   2nd row – Crochet another double crochet all the way around the edge.
   3rd row – Double crochet into the first stitch, * 4 chain, miss 2 double crochet, 2 treble into the next double crochet, 4 chain, 2 treble into the same stitch, 4 chain, miss 2 double crochet, 1 double crochet into the next stitch, repeat from *.

To complete scissor case:

1. Lay the crocheted front scissor case onto the crocheted back. The back embroidery should be facing away from you. With a thread of crochet cotton and a sewing needle, stitch the front scissor case to the back scissor case. Make sure you secure your first and last stitch very well as this will be a stress point. I use a stab stitch method, which is just a stitch up through the top fabric and back down through the back fabric. Make your stitches small as you want the case to be secure.

2. Sew a button on the front of the tab, 12 mm ($^{1}/2"$) down from the crocheted edge.

3. You might like to add a tassel to your scissor case. All the tassels used for this project were made by Su-Lee Oei.

## Needle Threader Case

To embroider front section:

Trace the front needle threader shape on page 105 onto a piece of woollen fabric. Cut two front shapes (but you will only embroider one). Do not cut the exact size as this is a small item and would be very hard to embroider.
   Now transfer the design on the needle threader pattern to the fabric.

1. Embroider stem stitch roses 1 and 2 first using Kirra yarns Mohair No. 324.

2. Embroider rose 3 using Kirra yarns Mohair No. 325.

3. Embroider the fly stitch rose leaves next using Kirra yarns Mohair No. 216.

4. Embroider the straight stitch stems at the bottom of the roses using Kirra yarns Mohair No. 216.

5. Embroider the buds on the straight stitch stems (one colonial knot on each stem) using Patina No. PA257.

6. Embroider the side buds at the top using Kirra Yarns Mohair No. 326. The buds are colonial knots.

7. Embroider the fine stems and sew on the beads, following steps 12 and 13 of the instructions for embroidering the front of the pin cushion, page 98.

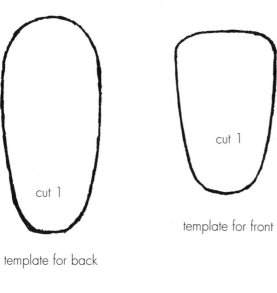

cut 1

template for back

cut 1

template for front

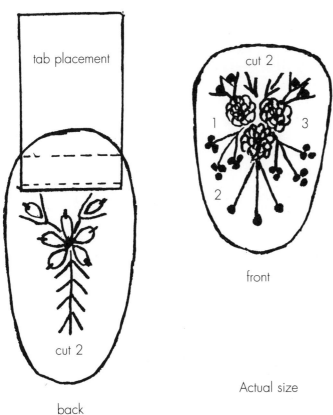

tab placement

cut 2

1    3

2

front

cut 2

back

Actual size

Patterns and embroidery for needle threader case

To embroider back section:

Cut two pieces of woollen fabric using the back pattern on page 108. Again, cut each piece larger than the pattern, as it would be difficult to embroider such a small item.
    Transfer the design on the pattern to the fabric.

1. Embroider the cream lazy daisy flower in Kirra yarns Mohair No. 331. Embroider the buds in the same wool. Each bud is one lazy daisy petal.

2. Embroider the continuous fly stitch fern using Patina No. PA136. Embroider one fly stitch around the bud.

3. Embroider small straight stitches over the ends of the lazy daisy petals and the buds with Patina No. PA136.

4. Embroider one colonial knot in the centre of each lazy daisy flower using Patina No. PA136.

To assemble, crochet and complete threader case:

The needle threader case is crocheted and sewn together in the same way as the scissor case. Follow the instructions on pages 102 and 104. Once again, you might like to add a tassel to your needle threader case.

## Needle Book

To embroider needle book cover:

Cut two pieces of woollen fabric using the cover pattern on page 108. I would suggest you cut the fabric larger than the pattern so that it is easier to machine around. You can cut the excess fabric away after you have machined it. Mark the needle book cover outline with a water soluble pen.
    Transfer the design on the cover pattern to the fabric. Fold the fabric to make sure the front design falls in the centre of the front of the needle book cover, and the back design in the centre of the back.

1. Embroider roses 1, 2, 3 and 4 first using Kirra yarns Mohair No. 324.

2. Embroider roses 5 and 6 using Kirra yarns Mohair No. 325.

3. Embroider the fly stitch rose leaves using Kirra yarns Mohair No. 216.

4. Embroider the straight stitch stems at the top and bottom of the roses using Kirra yarns Mohair No. 216.

5. Embroider the buds on the straight stitch stems (one colonial knot on each stem) using Patina No. PA257.

6. Embroider the side buds top and bottom using Kirra yarns Mohair No. 326. The buds are worked in colonial knots.

7. Embroider the fly stitch around the buds using Kirra yarns Mohair No. 216. Take the fly stitch stem back to the rose to form the stem of the bud.

8. Embroider the cream lazy daisy flowers using Kirra yarns Mohair No. 331. Embroider the buds in the same wool. Each bud is one lazy daisy petal.

9. Embroider the continuous fly stitch fern using Patina No. PA136. Embroider one fly stitch around the bud.

10. Embroider small straight stitches over the ends of the lazy daisy petals and the buds with Patina No PA136.

11. Embroider one colonial knot in the centre of each lazy daisy flower using Patina No. PA136.

12. Embroider the fine stems and sew on the beads, following steps 12 and 13 of the instructions for embroidering the front of the pin cushion, page 98.

To assemble and crochet needle book cover:

Cut two pieces of template plastic using the template cover pattern on page 108.

1. Take the embroidered needle book and one of the tabs without a buttonhole in it and position the tab as shown on the cover pattern on page 108. Pin the tab in place and sew on by machine across the folded edge of the tab. The crocheted edge should be on the top. You can sew a second row of stitching 5 mm (1/4") above the previous row of stitching.

2. Lay the plain piece of woollen fabric down on the table. Now lay the embroidered cover with the embroidery facing up on top of the template plastic. The template plastic will be sandwiched between both pieces of woollen fabric. Pin both fabrics together around the markings. It is also a good idea to tack these two pieces of fabric together so that the template plastic will not slip when you are machining around it.

3. After you have machined around the needle book cover, cut the excess fabric away leaving a 3 mm (1/8") seam allowance from the machine stitching.

4. Using DMC Perle 8 crochet cotton ecru and a .6 mm crochet hook, crochet all around the cover:
1st row – 1 double crochet all the way around.
2nd row – 1 double crochet into the first stitch, * 4 chain, miss 2 double crochet, 2 treble into the next double crochet, 4 chain, 2 treble into the same stitch, 4 chain, miss 2 double crochet, 1 double crochet into the next stitch, repeat from *.

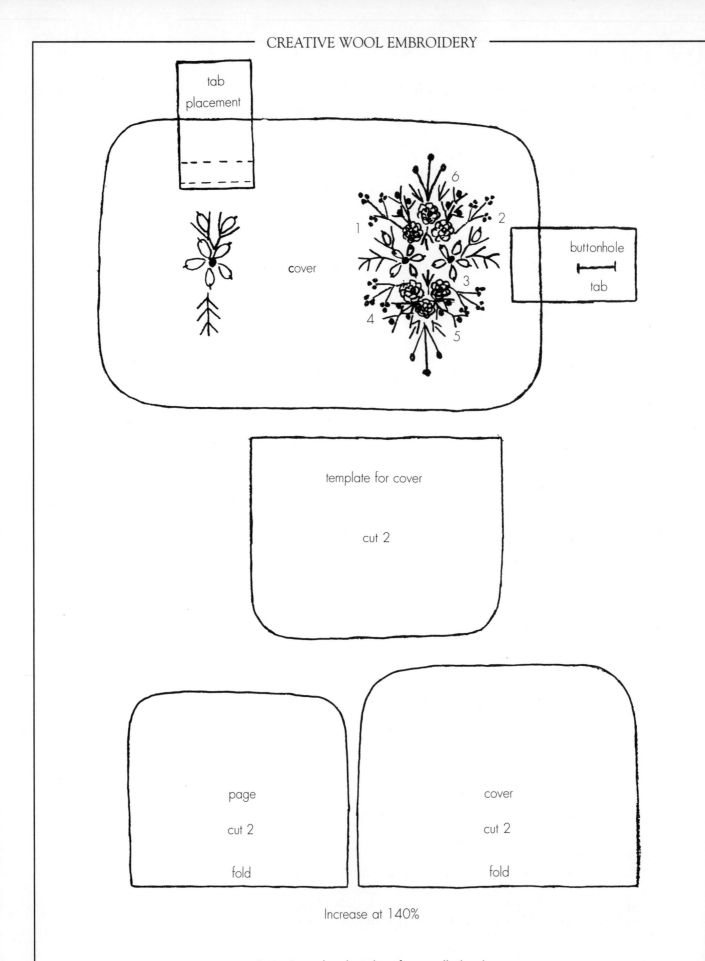

tab
placement

cover

6

2

1

3

4

5

buttonhole

tab

template for cover

cut 2

page

cut 2

fold

cover

cut 2

fold

Increase at 140%

Patterns and embroidery for needle book

To complete needle book:

1. Hand sew one tab with a buttonhole in it onto the inside cover of the needle book in the centre.

2. Sew a button on the front of the plain tab 12 mm ($^1/_2$") down from the crocheted edge. Sew another button to the back cover in the centre to enable you to close your needle book.

3. Cut two pieces of woollen fabric the size of the needle book page pattern (page 108). Pin together and machine around the edge, 3 mm ($^1/_8$") in from the edge. No template plastic is required in this page.

4. Crochet around the page following step 4 on page 107.

5. Place this page on top of the needle book cover with the embroidery facing down. Pin through the centre of the cover and the page. You will find your template plastic will part to make way for the pins. Hand tack the two together and then machine both together.

6. You may like to add a tassel to your needle book.

**Thimble Case**

To embroider side pieces of thimble case:

Trace the thimble case shape on page 110 onto the woollen fabric with a water soluble pen. Cut three – two sides and one back. Do not cut them out to size, as it will be very difficult to machine around them. Leave a good size seam allowance, about 2.5 cm (1").

Tranfer the side design on page 110 to each of the two side pieces.

1. Embroider stem stitch roses 1 and 2 using Kirra yarns Mohair No. 324.

2. Embroider rose 3 next using Kirra yarns Mohair No. 325.

3. Embroider the fly stitch rose leaves using Kirra yarns Mohair No. 216.

4. Embroider the straight stitch stems at the top and bottom of the roses using Kirra yarns Mohair No. 216.

5. Embroider the side bottom buds using Kirra yarns Mohair No. 326. Each bud is one colonial knot.

6. Embroider the buds on the straight stems using Patina No. PA257. Embroider one colonial knot on each stem.

7. Embroider the fly stitch around the side buds using Kirra yarns Mohair No. 216. Take the fly stitch stem back to the rose to form the stem of the bud.

8. Embroider the fine stems and sew on the beads, following steps 12 and 13 in the instructions for embroidering the front of the pin cushion, page 98.

Embroider the other side of the thimble case in the same manner as this one.

To embroider back of thimble case:

Transfer the back design below to the third piece of woollen fabric.

1. Embroider the cream lazy daisy flowers first using Kirra yarns Mohair No. 331. Embroider the buds in the same wool. Each bud consists of one lazy daisy petal.

2. Embroider the continuous fly stitch fern using Patina No. PA136. Embroider one fly stitch around the bud.

3. Embroider small straight stitches over the ends of the lazy daisy petals and the buds with Patina No. PA136.

4. Embroider one colonial knot in the centre of each lazy daisy flower using Patina No. PA136.

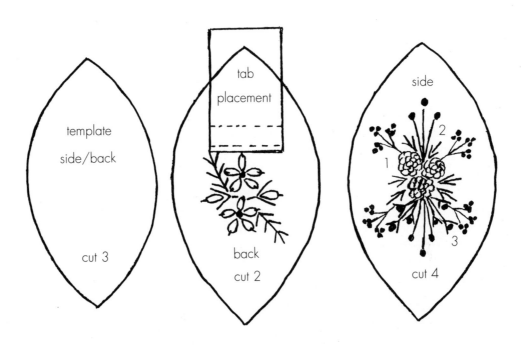

Increase at 140%

Patterns and embroidery for thimble case

To assemble and crochet sides:

Cut three pieces of template plastic using the pattern on page 110. Cut two pieces of woollen fabric bigger than the thimble sides. There is no need to mark out the shape beforehand.

1. On the table lay a piece of plain woollen fabric, then a piece of template plastic and then place one of the side thimble case pieces on top with the embroidery facing up. The template plastic is now sandwiched between the two pieces of woollen fabric. Pin and then hand tack around the case markings. Now machine around the markings.

2. Cut away the excess fabric leaving a 3 mm ($1/8$") seam allowance from the machine stitching. Make the other side in the same manner.

3. Crochet all around one of the sides, using DMC Perle 8 crochet cotton and a .6 mm crochet hook:
   1st row – 1 double crochet all the way around.
   2nd row – Crochet another row of double crochet all the way around.
   3rd row – 1 double crochet into the first stitch, * 4 chain, miss 2 double crochet, 2 treble into the next double crochet, 4 chain, 2 treble into the same stitch, 4 chain, miss 2 double crochet, 1 double crochet into the next stitch, repeat from * .

Follow the same instructions for the other heavily embroidered side.

To assemble and crochet back:

1. Take the embroidered back piece and one of your tabs without a buttonhole in it and position the tab as shown on the back pattern on page 110. Pin the tab in place and sew on by machine across the folded edge of the tab. The crocheted edge should be on the top. You can sew a second row of stitching 5 mm ($1/4$") above the previous row of stitching.

2. Take one piece of plain woollen fabric bigger than the back pattern, and the embroidered back piece. Pin them together with the embroidery facing up and the template plastic sandwiched in between. Hand tack the fabric around the markings and then machine all the way around.

3. Cut away excess fabric leaving a 3 mm ($1/8$") seam allowance from the machine stitching.

4. With DMC Perle No. 8 crochet cotton and a .6 mm crochet hook, crochet around the back:
   1st row – 1 double crochet all the way around.
   2nd row – Crochet another row of double crochet all the way around the edge.
   (You do not crochet a fancy edge on this piece.)

5. Sew a button on the front of the tab 12 mm ($^1$/$_2$") down from the crocheted edge.

To complete thimble case:

1. Take one heavy embroidered side and stab stitch one side only to the back piece. Stab stitching is just a stitch up through the top fabric and back down through the back fabric. Make sure you secure the first and last stitch well. I have used crochet cotton to sew the case together.

2. Take the second heavily embroidered side and stab stitch one side only to the back piece. You should have an opening in the middle of the two sides. Note that the embroidery on the sides should be facing the same way. The buds are different top and bottom.

3. If you like, you can add a tassel to the bottom of your thimble case.

**Tape Measure Bag**

To embroider tape measure bag:

Cut the tape measure bag out of woollen fabric using the pattern on page 113. Check the pattern for the positions of the buttonholes. They must measure 12 mm ($^1$/$_2$") in length.
Cut the buttonholes now.
  Transfer the designs on the tape measure bag pattern to the fabric.

1. Embroider roses 1 and 2 using Kirra yarns Mohair No. 324.

2. Embroider rose 3 next using Kirra yarns Mohair No. 325.

3. Embroider the fly stitch rose leaves using Kirra yarns Mohair No. 216.

4. Embroider the straight stitch stems at the top and bottom of the roses using Kirra yarns Mohair No. 216.

5. Embroider the side bottom buds using Kirra yarns Mohair No. 326. Each bud consists of one colonial knot.

6. Embroider the fly stitch around the side bottom buds using Kirra yarns Mohair No. 216. Take the fly stitch stem back to the rose to form the stem of the bud.

7. Embroider the fine stems and sew on the beads, following steps 12 and 13 of the instructions for embroidering the front of the pin cushion, page 98.

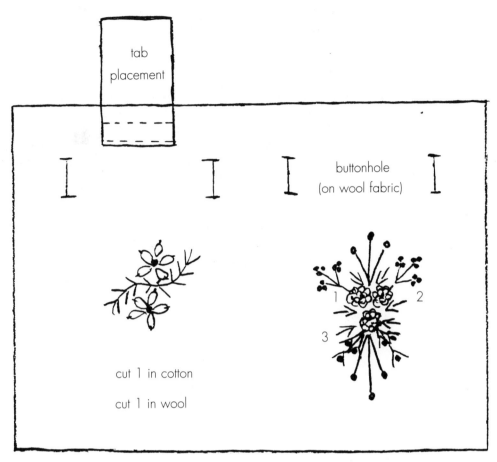

Increase at 140%

**Pattern and embroidery for tape measure bag**

To assemble and crochet tape measure bag:

Cut a piece of fine cotton fabric the same size as the woollen fabric. This is the lining for the bag.

1. Take one of the tabs without a buttonhole in it and position the tab as shown on the pattern above. Pin the tab in place and machine on across the folded edge only. You can sew a second row of stitching 5 mm ($^1/4$") above the previous row of stitching.

2. With right sides of fabric facing each other, machine the side seam and bottom edge of the woollen bag. Seams of 5 mm ($^1/4$") have been allowed. Turn the bag to the right side.

3. Sew the cotton fabric in the same manner.

4. Do not turn the cotton fabric bag to the right side, just slip it inside the woollen bag. Pin both edges together around the top, and machine a line of stitching 3 mm ($^1/8$") in from the edge.

5. Work the crochet in DMC Perle 8 crochet cotton ecru and a .6 mm crochet hook. Crochet all around the top of your bag:
1st row – 1 double crochet into each hole.
2nd row – 1 double crochet into the first stitch, * 4 chain, miss 2 double crochet, 2 treble into the next double crochet, 4 chain, 2 treble into the same stitch, 4 chain, miss 2 double crochet, 1 double crochet into the next stitch, repeat from *.

To complete tape measure bag:

1. The bag is too small to sew by machine, and so you will have to hand sew the casing for the ties. Mark a line for your stitching 1.5 cm (5/8") down from the top of the woollen fabric. Mark a second row 2 cm (3/4") down from the previous marking. Using the crochet cotton in a No. 20 chenille needle, embroider a whipped chain around these markings. Make sure you take your stitches through both layers of fabric.

2. Using a small safety pin, thread one piece of cord or double-sided ribbon through the buttonhole, and then through the casing to come out at the buttonhole next to where you started. Tie both ends together in a knot.

3. Take the other cord and thread it through the opposite buttonhole, coming out at the buttonhole next to where you started. Tie both ends together in a knot. Draw both ends of cord up to close the bag.

4. Sew a button on the front of the tab 12 mm (1/2") down from the crocheted edge.

## Chatelaine Belt

To embroider belt:

Cut two pieces of woollen fabric using the pattern on page 115. It is a good idea to add an extra seam of 12 mm (1/2") to make machining around the belt easier. You will cut this fabric back to 3 mm (1/8") once you have machined it.

Transfer the design on the belt pattern to the fabric. With this piece I would suggest you transfer small sections at a time.

1. Embroider the whipped chain border first using Kirra yarns Mohair No. 330.

2. Embroider your initial next using Kirra yarns Mohair No. 330 and whipped chain. You can draw your own initial or trace one from an initial book. You can also embroider a couple of stem stitch roses in your initial, poisitoning them wherever you like. I embroidered one rose in Kirra yarns Mohair No. 324 and the other in Kirra yarns Mohair No. 325.

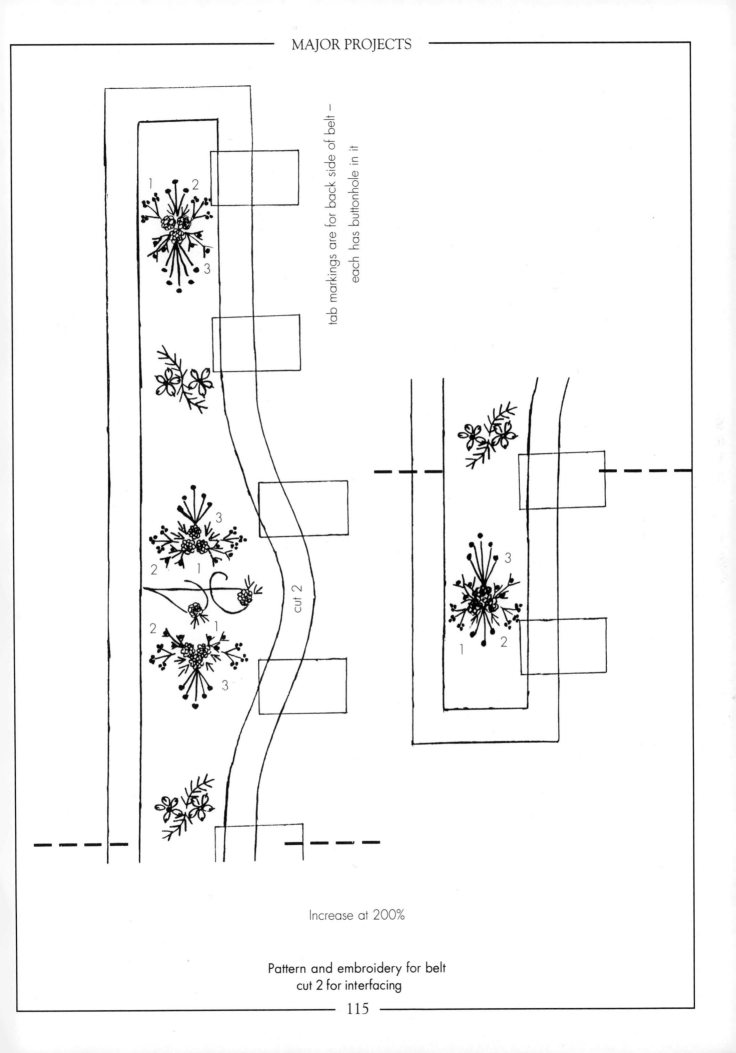

tab markings are for back side of belt –

each has buttonhole in it

cut 2

Increase at 200%

Pattern and embroidery for belt
cut 2 for interfacing

3. Embroider the rose section around your initial. Work rose 1 and 2 first using Kirra yarns Mohair No. 324.

4. Embroider rose 3 next using Kirra yarns Mohair No. 325.

5. Embroider the fly stitch rose leaves using Kirra yarns Mohair No. 216.

6. Embroider the inside buds near your initial using Kirra yarns Mohair No. 326. Each bud consists of a colonial knot.

7. Embroider the fly stitch around the buds next using Kirra yarns Mohair No. 216. Take the fly stitch stem back to the rose to form the stem of the bud.

8. Embroider the straight stitch stems at the side of the roses using Kirra yarns Mohair No. 216.

9. Embroider the colonial knot buds on the straight stitch stems using Patina No. PA257.

10. Embroider the fine stems and sew on the beads, following steps 12 and 13 of the instructions for embroidering the front of the pin cushion, page 98.

11. Reverse this section on the other side of your initial.

12. Embroider the cream lazy daisy flowers on both sides using Kirra yarns Mohair No. 331.

13. Embroider the continuous fly stitch fern using Patina No. PA136.

14. Embroider small straight stitches over the ends of the lazy daisy petals with Patina No. PA136.

15. Embroider one colonial knot in the centre of each lazy daisy flower using Patina No. PA136.

16. Embroider the outer rose section next. Embroider roses 1 and 2 using Kirra yarns Mohair No. 324.

17. Embroider rose 3 using Kirra yarns Mohair No. 325.

18. Embroider the fly stitch rose leaves using Kirra yarns Mohair No. 216.

19. Embroider the straight stitch stems both sides of the roses using Kirra yarns Mohair No. 216.

20. Embroider the buds on the straight stitch stems using Patina No. PA257 (one colonial knot on each stem).

21. Embroider the fine stems and sew on the beads.

22. Embroider the second set of roses on the other side, which will be the reverse of this side.

To assemble and crochet chatelaine belt:

1. Sew on the crocheted tabs with the buttonholes in them to the back of the chatelaine belt, in the positions shown on the belt pattern (page 115). Pin the tabs in place and machine across the folded edge only. You can sew a second row of stitching 5 mm ($^1$/4") above the previous row of stitching.

2. Cut two pieces of interfacing using the belt pattern with the extra seam allowance added on. Hand tack these two pieces of interfacing together.

3. On the table, lay the back of the chatelaine belt, with the wrong side facing up, then the two pieces of interfacing tacked together. On top, lay the front embroidered chatelaine belt, with the embroidery facing up. Pin all the layers together. The outline of the chatelaine belt should be marked.

4. Machine around the chatelaine belt on the marking line. Cut away the excess fabric, leaving a 3 mm ($^1$/8") seam allowance.

5. Follow step 5 of the instructions 'To assemble and crochet tape measure bag', page 114. Crochet all around the chatelaine belt.

To complete chatelaine belt:

Cut two pieces of woollen fabric, 40 cm x 10 cm (15 $^3$/4" x 4"), for the ties.

1. Fold the ties in half, pin together and machine down the long side and across the bottom with a 5 mm ($^1$/4") seam. Leave one end open to push the tie through. Make two of these ties in the same way. Iron the ties once you have turned them through.

2. Machine the ties to the front chatelaine belt near the crocheted edge. You will have to centre the ties on the belt as they are not the same width as the belt. You will also have to adjust the ties to your waist size. Do not have the belt too tight.

3. Machine one buttonhole in the right-hand tie, 2.5 cm (1") in from the edge. The size of the buttonhole will depend on the size of your buttons. My buttonhole measures 12 mm ($^1$/2"). Make sure your button will go through the buttonhole.

4. Sew two buttons on the left-hand tie. Sew one button according to your waist size and sew the other button so that you can let the chatelaine out if you wish.

5. It is now time to button all the chatelaine pieces onto the belt. Position the pieces in whatever order you would like them.

*Greeting card* _____

REQUIREMENTS

**Materials:**
Woollen fabric, 10 cm x 13 cm (4" x 5")
No. 20 chenille needles
No. 10 crewel needles
Mill Hill glass seed beads No. 00151

**Threads:**
Kirra yarns Mohair
– Nos 324, 325, 326 and 216
DMC stranded cotton No. 524
Patina No. PA257

*Note:* If you have completed the Pin Cushion, Needle Book or Chatelaine, you should have enough yarns.

**Stitches used:**
Stem stitch, fly stitch, straight stitch and colonial knots.

With a water soluble pen, draw the outline of the opening of the card on the piece of woollen fabric. Transfer the design to your fabric.

1. Embroider stem stitch roses 1 and 2 first using Kirra yarns Mohair No. 324.

2. Embroider rose 3 using Kirra yarns Mohair No. 325.

3. Embroider the fly stitch rose leaves using Kirra yarns Mohair No. 216.

4. Embroider the straight stitch stems at the top and bottom of the roses using Kirra yarns Mohair No. 216.

5. Embroider the side buds out from the bottom of the roses using Kirra yarns Mohair No. 326. The buds are worked in colonial knots.

6. Embroider the fly stitch around the buds using Kirra yarns Mohair No. 216. Take the fly stitch stem back to the rose to form the stem of the bud.

7. Embroider the top and bottom buds on the straight stitch stems (one colonial knot on each stem) using Patina No. PA257.

8. Embroider the fine stems using one strand of DMC stranded cotton No. 524. These stems consist of one fly stitch with a stem and one straight stitch in the centre.

9. Sew three Mill Hill glass seed beads No. 00151 on the tip of each fine stem. Sew each bead on separately. Each set of fine stems has three sets of three beads, nine beads in total.

To make up the greeting card, refer to the instructions on page 49.

*actual size*

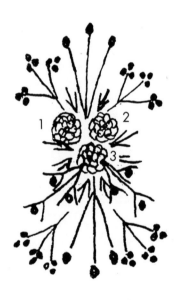

Stem Stitch Roses and Buds –
Greeting Card

## SUNFLOWERS

*Blanket*

This blanket is large enough to use as a throwover on a single bed. But wherever you place these sunflowers, they are sure to make an eye-catching display.

REQUIREMENTS

**Materials:**
Wool blanketing,
– 1 piece, 106 cm x 80 cm (41 $^3$/4" x 31 $^1$/2") for central panel
– 4 pieces, each 31 cm x 31 cm (12 $^1$/4") for corner squares
– 2 pieces, each 73.5 cm x 28 cm (29" x 11") for short borders
– 2 pieces, each 1 m x 28 cm (39" x 11") for long borders
Green and bone striped cotton fabric, 120 cm (47") length
Quilter's cream muslin, 170 cm (67") x 150 cm (59") wide
No. 18 chenille needles

**Threads:**
Appletons tapestry wool
– 2 skeins Nos 347, 474, 693, 472 and 843
– 8 skeins No. 345
Anchor tapestry wool
– 2 skeins No. 9642
– 3 skeins No. 9496
– 8 skeins No. 8018
Semco tapestry wool No. 636 (3 skeins)
Leah's No. 305
DMC Perle 5 No. 676 (2 skeins)
Little Wood Fleece yarns 3 ply Gossamer mohair No. 7
    Br/Orange (2 skeins)
DMC Perle 3
– Nos 726 and 676
DMC stranded cotton No. 310
Stonehouse Paterna wool No. 262

**Stitches used:**
Colonial knots, lazy daisy stitch, straight stitch, buttonhole stitch, coral stitch, back stitch, whipped chain stitch, satin stitch and bullion stitch.

To embroider central panel:

Transfer the design on the insert to the central panel of wool blanketing. Transfer one section at a time. Mark all the centres of the sunflowers first.

1. Embroider all the inner centres of the sunflower first using Appletons tapestry wool No. 347. These inner centres are filled with colonial knots packed in very tightly.

2. Embroider all the outer circles of the sunflower centres using Anchor tapestry wool No. 9642. Each circle consists of one row of colonial knots.

3. Embroider the rest of the centre in all the sunflowers with Anchor tapestry wool No. 9496 and colonial knots. Pack the knots in tightly.

4. *Flower 1* Embroider the first row of petals using Appletons tapestry wool No. 474 and large lazy daisy stitches. Work the petals close together around the centre of the sunflower and make the holding stitch at the end of the petals longer to give a petal effect.

   Embroider one straight stitch in the centre of each lazy daisy petal using Appletons tapestry wool No. 693.

   Using Appletons tapestry wool No. 474, embroider another row of lazy daisy stitches around the first row, going in between the petals of the previous row. Extend the holding stitch as before.

   Embroider one straight stitch in the centre of each lazy daisy petal using Anchor tapestry wool No. 8018.

5. *Flower 2* Follow the instructions for flower 1, using the wools specified below:
   1st row of petals – Anchor tapestry wool No. 8018. Straight stitch in centre of each petal – Appletons tapestry wool No. 693.
   2nd row of petals – Anchor tapestry wool No. 8018. Straight stitch in centre of each petal – Semco tapestry wool No. 636.

6. *Flower 3* Follow the instructions for flower 1, using the wools specified below:
   1st row of petals – ·Anchor tapestry wool No. 8018. Straight stitch in centre of each petal – Appletons tapestry wool No. 474.
   2nd row of petals – Anchor tapestry wool No. 8018. Straight stitch in centre of each petal – Semco tapestry wool No. 636.

7. *Flower 4* Follow the instructions for flower 1, using the wools specified below:
   1st row of petals – Appletons tapestry wool No. 472. Straight stitch in centre of each petal – Appletons tapestry wool No. 843.
   2nd row of petals – Appletons tapestry wool No. 472. Straight stitch in centre of each petal – Anchor tapestry wool No. 8018.

8. *Flower 5* Follow the instructions for flower 1, using the wools specified below:
   1st row of petals – Appletons tapestry wool No. 472. Straight stitch in centre of each petal – Appletons tapestry wool No. 474.
   2nd row of petals – Appletons tapestry wool No. 472 Straight stitch in centre of each petal – Anchor tapestry wool No. 8018.

9. *Flower 6* Follow the instructions for flower 1, using the wools specified below:
   1st row of petals – Anchor tapestry wool No. 8018. Straight stitch in centre of each petal – Appletons tapestry wool No. 843.
   2nd row of petals – Anchor tapestry wool No. 8018. Straight stitch in centre of each petal – Semco tapestry wool No. 636.

10. Embroider the sunflower pods for the buds using Appletons tapestry wool No. 345. The pods are worked in large buttonhole stitch.

11. Embroider the bud petals using Anchor tapestry wool No. 8018. The petals are large lazy daisy stitches with the holding stitch extended to give the effect of a petal.

12. Embroider one straight stitch in the centre of each petal using Appletons tapestry wool No. 843.

13. Embroider another row of lazy daisy petals above the first row, going in between the petals of the previous row. Use Anchor tapestry wool No. 8018. The petals are large lazy daisy stitches with the holding stitch extended.

14. Embroider one straight stitch in the centre of each petal using Appletons tapestry wool No. 843.

15. Embroider the stems to the sunflowers and buds using Appletons tapestry wool No. 347 and coral stitch.

16. Transfer all the leaves. Outline the leaves with a large back stitch using Appletons tapestry wool No. 345. Next embroider the straight stitches that are angled out from each join of the back stitch. The length of the stitch is 5 mm ($^{1}/_{4}$").

17. Transfer the veins of the leaves. Embroider a back stitch up the centre vein first using Appletons tapestry wool No. 345. Work straight stitches of various lengths out from the joins of the back stitches.

18. Embroider five straight stitches at the bottom of each of the large leaves using Appletons tapestry wool No. 345. On the smaller leaves embroider only three straight stitches using the same wool.

19. Embroider one straight stitch from the five or three straight stitches at the bottom of the leaves using Appletons tapestry wool No. 347. This stitch should be taken back to the main stem.

20. Transfer the bow. Embroider the bow using Leah's No. 305 and whipped chain stitch.

21. Transfer the wheat stems. Embroider the wheat stems in whipped chain stitch using DMC Perle 5 No. 676.

22. Transfer the wheat ears. Embroider the wheat ears using two strands of Little Wood Fleece yarns – 3 ply Gossamer Mohair No. 7 Br/Orange and lazy daisy stitch.

23. Embroider the straight stitches extending out from the wheat ears using DMC Perle 5 No. 676. The straight stitches are 2 cm (³/4") in length.

24. Embroider the bees next. Check the flower guide for instructions on how to embroider the bee.

To embroider four corner squares:

*Note:* It is a good idea to try to embroider the outer circles of the sunflower centres and at least one row of petals on all four squares in the one day. The reason for this is that your tension and length of stitch can vary from day to day. It is very important that the four corners are the same size. The second row of lazy daisy petals, the colonial knots in the centre of the sunflowers and the leaves can all be embroidered at a later date.

Transfer the markings for the centres of all the sunflowers to the corner squares using a water soluble pen. The design for the corner squares is on page 123.

1. Embroider all the outer circles of the sunflower centres. (The inner centres can be embroidered at a later date.) The outline consists of one row of colonial knots embroidered in Anchor tapestry wool No. 9642.

2. Embroider the first row of sunflower petals using Anchor tapestry wool No. 8018. Each petal is a large lazy daisy stitch with a long holding stitch at the end to give a petal effect. Embroider the petals close together around the centre of the sunflower.

3. Embroider one straight stitch in the centre of each lazy daisy petal using Appletons tapestry wool No. 693.

4. Embroider the second row of lazy daisy petals around the first row, going in between the petals of the first row. Use Anchor tapestry wool No. 8018 for the petals and extend the holding stitch as before.

5. Embroider one straight stitch in the centre of each lazy daisy petal using Semco tapestry wool No. 636.

6. Embroider the inner centres of the sunflowers using Appletons tapestry wool No. 347. Each centre is filled with colonial knots packed in very tightly.

7. Embroider the rest of the centres in all the sunflowers with Anchors tapestry wool No. 9496 and tightly packed colonial knots.

Increase at 130%

Embroidery for corner square

8. Transfer all the leaves. Outline the leaves with a large back stitch first using Appletons tapestry wool No. 345. Next embroider the straight stitches angled out from each join of the back stitch. The stitch length is 5 mm ($^1/4$").

9. Transfer the veins of the leaves. Using Appletons tapestry wool No. 345, embroider a back stitch up the centre vein first. Embroider straight stitches of various lengths out from the joins of the back stitches.

10. Embroider five straight stitches at the bottom of the leaves using Appletons tapestry wool No. 345.

11. Embroider the sunflower stems in coral stitch using Appletons tapestry wool No. 347.

12. Embroider one straight stitch from the five straight stitches at the bottom of each leaf using Appletons tapestry wool No. 347. This stitch should be taken back to the main stem.

To embroider borders:

There are two short borders and two long borders. Transfer the design on page 125 onto the blanket borders. The shorter border has one less scallop.

1. Embroider the scallops first in whipped chain using DMC Perle 5 No. 676. Note that the whipping stitch is embroidered with DMC Perle 3 No. 676.

2. Transfer the leaves. Outline the leaves with a long back stitch using Appletons tapestry wool No. 345. Next embroider the straight stitches that are angled out from each join of the back stitch. The length of the stitch is about 3 mm ($^1/8$").

3. Transfer the veins of the leaves. Embroider a back stitch up the centre vein first using Appletons tapestry wool No. 345. Embroider straight stitches of various lengths out from the joins of the back stitch.

4. *Small sunflowers* Embroider the first row of petals around the sunflower centre with medium-length lazy daisy stitches, extending the holding stitch at the bottom of the petal. Use Anchor tapestry wool No. 8018.

   Embroider another row of lazy daisy petals around the first row, going in between the petals of the previous row and using Anchor tapestry wool No. 8018. Extend the holding stitch out as before.

   Embroider one colonial knot only in the centre of each flower using Appletons tapestry wool No. 347.

   Embroider colonial knots around the centre knot using Anchor tapestry wool No. 9496.

The shorter border has one less scallop

Increase at 200%

Embroidery for border section

Note that only one-half of the design for the long border is shown here (use three scallops)

To assemble sunflower blanket:

Wash the striped fabric and the backing fabric first, and then iron when dry.

1. Cut the striped fabric on the bias. Cut three strips 5 cm (2") wide and the full length of the bias. To find the bias, fold the left-hand bottom corner over to the top right-hand corner (diags 1 and 2). Cut along the fold.

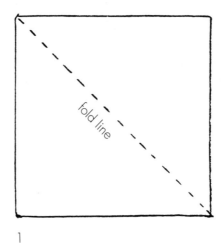

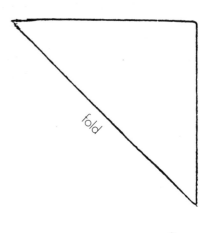

1      2

2. Bind the two edges of each of the four corner squares with the bias strips.

    Place the edge of the blanketing and the edge of the bias strip together, right sides facing (diag. 3). Machine a line of stitching through both fabrics 8 mm (3/8") from the raw edges. Do not overstretch the bias when sewing.

    Hand tack the binding back on the four corner squares (diag. 4).

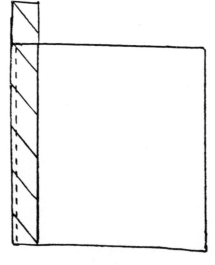

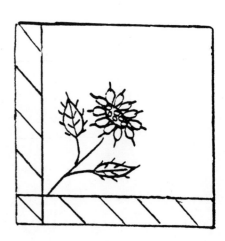

3      4

3. Lay the two long and two short borders out on a table or floor.

4. With a water soluble pen, mark the borders 2.25 cm ($^7/_8$") in from the edge (diag. 5).

5. Lay the four square corners on top of the borders.

6. Place the edge of the tacked-back binding on the 2.25 cm markings and pin in place. Machine the four corners on down the two edges that have the binding on them. Machine very close to the binding and the wool, or in the ditch (diag. 7). It is very important that you machine very close to the binding because you only have a limited amount of fabric underneath to machine through.

7. With a water soluble pen, mark all around the inner borders, 2.25 cm ($^7/_8$") in from the edge (diag. 6).

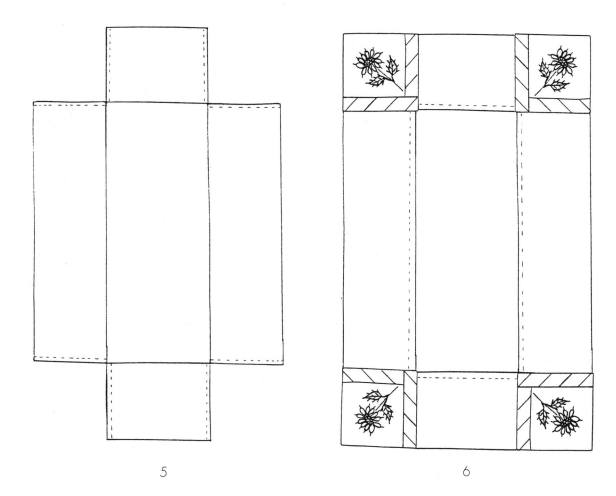

5                                          6

8. It is a good idea to round slightly the corners of the central panel. This makes it simpler to bind around the corners. Cut all corners on the central panel the same.

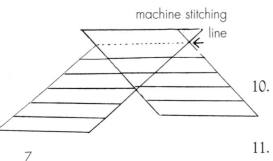

machine stitching line

7

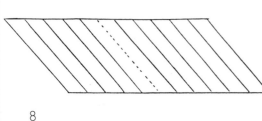

8

9. Cut three bias strips, 5 cm (2") wide and the full length of the bias, out of the striped fabric. Join the bias to create one strip.

   Cut the ends of both bias pieces of fabric along one stripe. Lay the two pieces together, right sides facing, and machine along a stripe (diag. 7). Your join should be unnoticeable (diag. 8). Iron the seam open.

10. Bind all around the central panel, starting the binding in the middle of one of the long sides. Hand tack the binding back.

11. Centre the central panel over the borders. Mark the halfway point on the panel. Pin in place and then machine very close to the binding and the wool.

12. Fold the washed backing fabric in half on the longest side. This gives you the centre of the fabric. Mark this centre with pins or a water soluble pen. Take the embroidered blanket and fold it in the centre on the longest side as well. Mark the centre with pins or a water soluble pen. Now is the time to round all four corners of the embroidered blanket to make them simpler to bind around.

13. Lay the backing fabric on a table or floor. Now lay the embroidered blanket, with the right side facing up, on top of the backing fabric. Make sure you lay the centres on top of one another. Pin and hand tack the two layers together. If you have an overlocker, you can overlock both edges together. If you do not have an overlocker, just bind the edges straight away.

14. Cut wider binding strips, 7.5 cm (3") wide, for the outer edges, and try to cut the strips as long as possible to avoid too many joins. The binding on the outer edges is sewn on double. After joining the strips where necessary, fold the resulting bias strip in half lengthways and iron a crease in the centre. Machine the binding onto the blanket and then turn the folded edge of the binding over and hand sew around it (diag. 9).

15. Secure the backing fabric to the blanketing through a few sunflowers. With a No. 9 crewel needle and cream sewing thread, catch a few sunflowers through the backing fabric with a couple of stab stitches. (Stab stitching is just a stitch up through the fabric and back down through the fabric.) End each stab stitch off securely.

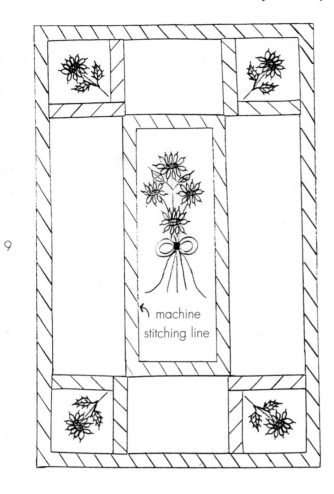

9

machine
stitching line

*Cushion* _____

REQUIREMENTS
**Materials:**
Wool blanketing, 39.5 cm x 39.5 cm (15 $^1/2$")
Cream cotton backing fabric, 45 cm (17 $^3/4$") length
Zipper, 35 cm (13 $^3/4$") long
Green and cream striped fabric, 50 cm length (19 $^3/4$")
Cushion insert, 45 cm x 45 cm (18") (the insert should be at
    least 2.5 cm, or 1", larger than the cushion)
No. 18 chenille needles

**Threads:**
Appletons tapestry wool
– Nos 347, 474, 693 and 345
Anchor tapestry wool
– Nos 9642, 9496 (2 skeins) and 8018 (2 skeins)
Semco tapestry wool No. 636
Leah's No. 305
DMC Perle 5 No. 676
Little Wood Fleece yarns 3 ply Gossamer Mohair No 7
    Br/Orange
DMC Perle 3 No. 726
DMC stranded cotton No. 310
Stonehouse Paterna wool No. 262

**Stitches used:**
Colonial knots, lazy daisy stitch, straight stitch, coral stitch, back stitch, whipped chain stitch, satin stitch and bullion stitch.

Transfer the design on page 131 to the cushion piece of wool blanketing. As this is a large design, transfer one section at a time. Mark all the centres of the sunflowers first.

1.  Embroider all the inner centres of the sunflowers first using Appletons tapestry wool No. 347. Fill the inner centres with colonial knots packed in tightly.

2.  Embroider all the outer circles of the sunflowers with Anchor tapestry wool No. 9642 and one row of colonial knots.

3.  Embroider the rest of the centre of all the sunflowers with Anchor tapestry wool No. 9496 and tightly packed colonial knots.

4.  *Flower 1*  Embroider the first row of large lazy daisy petals using Appletons tapestry wool No. 474. Work the petals close together around the centre of the flower and extend the holding stitch at the end of each petal to give a petal effect.
    Embroider one straight stitch in the centre of each lazy daisy petal using Appletons tapestry wool No. 693.
    Embroider another row of lazy daisy petals around the first row, going in between the petals of the previous row. Use Appletons tapestry wool No. 474 and extend the holding stitch as before.
    Embroider one straight stitch in the centre of each lazy daisy petal using Anchor tapestry wool No. 8018.

5.  *Flower 2*  Follow the instructions for flower 1, using the wools specified below:
    1st row of petals – Anchor tapestry wool No. 8018. Straight stitch in centre of each petal – Appletons tapestry wool No. 693.
    2nd row of petals – Anchor tapestry wool No. 8018. Straight stitch in centre of each petal – Semco tapestry wool No. 636.

6.  *Flower 3*  Follow the instructions for flower 1, using the wools specified below:
    1st row of petals – Anchor tapestry wool No. 8018. Straight stitch in centre of each petal – Appletons tapestry wool No. 474.
    2nd row of petals – Anchor tapestry wool No. 8018. Straight stitch in centre of each petal – Semco tapestry wool No. 636.

Increase at 200%

Sunflowers – Cushion

7. Embroider the sunflower stems in coral stitch using Appletons tapestry wool No. 347.

8. Transfer all the leaves. Outline the leaves with a large back stitch first using Appletons tapestry wool No. 345. Now embroider the straight stitches that are angled out from each join of the back stitch. The length of each stitch is 5 mm ($1/4$").

9. Transfer the veins of the leaves. Embroider a back stitch up the centre vein first using Appletons tapestry wool No. 345. Embroider straight stitches of various lengths out from the joins of the back stitch.

10. Embroider five straight stitches at the bottom of each leaf using Appletons tapestry wool No. 345.

11. Embroider one straight stitch from the five straight stitches at the bottom of the leaves using Appletons tapestry wool No. 347. This stitch should be taken back to the main stem.

12. Transfer the bow. Embroider the bow using Leah's No. 305 and whipped chain.

13. Transfer the wheat stems. Embroider the wheat stems in whipped chain using DMC Perle 5 No. 676.

14. Transfer the wheat ears and embroider using two strands of Little Wood Fleece Yarns 3 ply Gossamer Mohair No. 7 Br/Orange and lazy daisy stitch.

15. Embroider the straight stitch out from the wheat ears using DMC Perle 5 No. 676. The straight stitches are 2 cm ($3/4$") in length.

16. Embroider the bee. Check the flower guide for instructions on how to embroider the bee.

To make up the cushion:

Round the corners of the embroidered wool cushion piece to make it easier to pin on the frill. Cut two pieces of cream cotton fabric for the backing of the cushion, 39.5 cm x 22.5 cm (15 $1/2$" x 8 $3/4$").

1. Place the two backing pieces right sides together, and sew down 2 cm ($3/4$") from each end of the longest seam. Leave the middle section open for the zipper. The seam allowance is 2.5 cm (1"). Sew the 35 cm zipper in the opening of the seam.

2. Cut three pieces of striped cotton fabric for the frill, 15 cm x 115 cm (6" x 45").

3. Join the three pieces of frilling together to form a circle, allowing 12 mm ($1/2$") seams.

4. Fold the frill in half lengthways and iron a crease in the centre.

5. Start at a seam and sew two rows of gathering threads about 5 mm ($^1/4$") apart.

6. Mark the quarters of the embroidered cushion piece and the frill. Leave a pin in at the quarter marks on the cushion and the frill. Gather the frill to fit each quarter of the embroidered cushion.

7. Pin the frill around the outside of the cushion piece with the fold of the frill facing towards the centre of the cushion.

8. Machine the frill onto the woollen fabric, sewing 12 mm ($^1/2$") in from the edge of the frill. Remove the pins once you have sewn on the frill.

9. Take the backing piece of the cushion with the zipper in it and unzip the zip about 10 cm (4"). Place the right side of the wool cushion and the right side of the cotton backing piece together. Pin around the outside.

10. Turn the wool cushion over so that you can see the stitch line where you have just sewn on the frill. Machine around this stitch line.

11. Through the 10 cm zipper opening, lower the zip completely. You will be able to pull the cushion to the right side very easily through this opening.

12. Place the cushion cover over the cushion insert.

*Greeting Card*

REQUIREMENTS
Wool blanketing, 15 cm x 11.5 cm (6"x 4 $^1/2$")
Braid, enough to go around opening of card plus a small
    overlap
No. 18 chenille needles
Anchor tapestry wool
– Nos 8018, 9496, 345 and 347

*Note:* If you have made the Sunflower Blanket, you will not have to purchase any more wools.

Stitches used:
Lazy daisy, back stitch, straight stitch and colonial knots.

With a water soluble pen, draw the outline of the opening in the card on the piece of woollen fabric. This outline shows you how far you can take your embroidery out.

Remember that you have only a very small area to embroider on, therefore copy the design on the following page exactly.

1. Transfer the leaves to the greeting card blanketing first, and embroider using Appletons tapestry wool No. 345. Outline the leaves with a large back stitch. Then embroider the straight stitches that are angled out from each join of the back stitch. The length of the straight stitches is 5 mm ($^{1}/4$").

2. Transfer the veins of the leaves. Embroider a backstitch up the centre of the vein using Appletons tapestry wool No. 345. Embroider straight stitches of various lengths out from the joins of the back stitches.

3. Embroider the sunflower next. Embroider the first row of petals around the sunflower centre with Anchor tapestry wool No. 8018 and medium-length lazy daisy stitches. Extend the holding stitch at the bottom of the petal to give the effect of a petal.

   Embroider another row of lazy daisy petals around the first row, going in between the petals of the previous row. Use Anchor tapestry wool No. 8018 and extend the holding stitch out as before.

   Embroider one colonial knot only in the centre of the sunflower using Appletons tapestry wool No. 347.

   Embroider colonial knots around the centre knot using Anchor tapestry wool No. 9496.

To make up the greeting card, refer to the instructions on page 49. Glue the braid instead of lace around the opening on the front of the card.

*actual size*

**Sunflowers – Greeting Card**

All the projects in this book are available in kit form. If you would like a price list for the kits, please write, phone or fax. You will have to purchase the book for the instructions as the kits contain only the materials and threads.

Joan Watters is also available for workshops:

Joan Watters
Delwood Designs
PO Box 1294
Rozelle NSW 2039
Phone: (018) 248 989
Fax:     (02) 818 2856